Notes from the Catastrophic Realm

A Love Story

JUDITH HARROW

Copyright © 2011 Judith Harrow
All rights reserved.

ISBN: 1466481560
ISBN-13: 9781466481565

For every one of the friends, family, flora
and fauna whose grace and wisdom
guided me along the way,

and

in memory of my beloved husband, Arnold
Edward (Ted) Davidson and my cherished
auntie, Sylvia Katz Bauman; their light shines on.

Preface

When I was young I was spellbound by Edith Hamilton's books on Greek mythology. I wandered imaginatively, for hours on end, through the pantheon of Greek gods and goddesses, loving every one of them, considering them personal friends and advisors, but the one I loved best was Athena, goddess of wisdom, born fully-formed from the forehead of Zeus.

Then and there, I decided that wisdom was what I wanted most when I grew up, not money or fame or beauty, only wisdom. I wanted to become as wise, self-assured, and confident as Athena. I wanted to learn to put my finger on the pulse of the world, and I longed for the knowledge and discernment that I hoped would transform me into a happy, thriving adult.

Had I known better, had I not been such a naive and simple girl, I would never have made such a Faustian bargain with life. Wisdom, as I was later to learn, is not the daughter of love and beauty I imagined it to be. No, it is more often begot from a coupling of sorrow and despair, both of which extract a bitter price before yielding even the smallest morsel of treasure, but long ago, I knew none of that.

So I watched my younger brother sink into psychosis at age twenty, as my parents looked on in horror, and I first took notice of the indifferent nature of life. I later witnessed my father's death in increments from the systemic effects of diabetes, and as blindness, neuropathy, and kidney failure overcame him, the desolation I felt was occasionally accompanied by melancholy insights about the brutal finality of death.

In 1980, after surviving a near-death experience following minor gynecologic surgery, I learned something significant of the fragility of life, how it might end abruptly, in a single heartbeat, and

I began to comprehend its numinous beauty. And after my first husband Stefan died of a brain tumor at age forty-one, I lost too many years to anguish, sorrow, and self-destructive behavior, before coming upon a startling shaft of insight so bright, revelatory and unexpected that it changed the trajectory of my life.

I left my home in New York City settling with my cat Asia in a spacious apartment in the leafy town of Chapel Hill, North Carolina. I had saved a small sum of money, enough for a down payment on a modest home, but before I found the house I found a horse, a gray three-year-old gelding with a kind eye and an intelligent disposition. I realized how utterly foolish I would seem, squandering hard-earned money on something as impractical as a horse, but I bought Lucky anyway. It was one of the best decisions of my life, the realization of a childhood dream, and the beginning of a cherished relationship with an astonishing and beautiful being. The house had to wait another year.

One day, a friend asked if I wanted to meet her friend, an English professor, recently divorced, who had grown up on a cattle ranch in western Canada. Why not, I thought? So I met Ted one evening at a local cafe and was attracted to his quiet kindness, his quick-witted, perceptive demeanor, and the warm sparkle in his ice-blue eyes.

It wasn't an easy romance. Ted was eleven years older than I was and his divorce had left him feeling needy and bereft. Although I liked him, I felt bound by the seemingly ceaseless demands he made on my time and space. Eventually, I decided that despite aspects of Ted's personality and character I had so enjoyed, the relationship wasn't working, and I ended it.

Weeks later, while vacationing with my older brother Joel and his family in Colorado, I mentioned what had transpired with Ted. Joel was incredulous.

"You mean that you broke up with this man because he was paying too much attention to you, because he enjoyed being with you too much and wanted to talk to you every day? These are the things you found so objectionable? This is why you told him to go away?"

Joel advised that I talk to Ted about my feelings, something that, admittedly, I hadn't done. He suggested that my predicament with Ted might be worked through, and that it was prudent to think twice before turning my back on a man I truly liked and had begun to miss. He made good sense.

That night I phoned Ted from Colorado and we had a long, heartfelt conversation. Upon my return home, we took up where we left off and somehow the problems that had previously seemed so insurmountable simply disappeared. We soon began living together and, day by day, life became sweeter than I could ever have imagined. Seven years later we decided to marry, which we did in an intimate outdoor ceremony the following spring. Life was good and I was never happier. I fully expected that Ted and I would grow old together in our tranquil house by the lake, but life had something else in mind. Less than two years later our contented lives were shattered by the catastrophe that became the defining episode of my life, adding ruefully to my small store of wisdom, yet illustrating perfectly the profound, encompassing nature of love.

Me and Ted

November 24, 1997

It's been a week since Ted phoned me at work with the shattering news that he has pancreatic cancer. This isn't what we expected when he blithely drove himself to the hospital for a routine ultrasound exam. We had assumed his doctor's presumptive diagnosis of gallstones was correct. The ultrasound, we thought, was a mere formality, a way of providing visual evidence of his condition prior to treatment. But as it turned out, the doctor was wrong, and in an instant, our lives changed forever and we were thrust into the chaotic and frightening world of mortal illness. Nothing is the same as it once was, and I need to learn quickly how to accommodate to catastrophe.

This news has given me a new perspective on life or, more accurately, it has given me a multitude of perspectives which change shape and intensity with each erratic shift in my mood. It wills me to travel this road with Ted as a fully engaged participant. It causes me to want to leave this world with him whenever his end might come, to go home with him on the western wind, past the farthest star, and beyond all knowing. It makes me realize how dearly and desperately I love him. It has, in its own terrifying way, been a gift---this depth of knowing---but it is also the nightmare come real.

Perhaps we will be lucky. The report of Ted's needle biopsy indicates a tumor consistent with a cystic pancreatic neoplasm instead of the ordinary sort of pancreatic cancer which carries a survival rate of less than five percent. This cystic variety has a fifty percent survival rate, so the odds may be in our favor. Unfortunately, the diagnosis can't be definitively determined until the tumor is visualized during surgery, but at least there is the possibility, however slight, that Ted can survive this cancer and live out the full measure of his years.

Thanksgiving Day, November 27, 1997

My friend Alice, whom I've known for almost thirty years and love like a sister, is downstairs in our kitchen preparing a lavish Thanksgiving feast. She flew in from New York City several days ago because she thought Ted and I needed help feeling festive, or even mildly grateful. I suppose she's right. Mostly, we're numb: struck senseless from trying on the random fact of cancer that has settled on us like an ill-fitting garment. Celebrations of the season seem irrelevant right now, as the reality of Ted's cancer casts a dark shadow over everything, stifling my capacity for joy.

Still, it is a mild, bright November day and a slight breeze ripples across the lake. We are fortunate to live in this beautiful place. Our serene Japanese style house sits on a low rise that looks out on Lake Orange. Our cove is no longer the mosquito bearing mudflat it was last summer when drought reduced it to the volume and consistency of a large muddy puddle. Now, it is robust and voluptuous again, restored to fullness by rain and time. Filtered autumn sunlight bounces off the blue water which sparkles as though someone had tossed a bushel of diamonds onto the lake's surface. It's a restorative and soothing sight.

Early this morning Alice and I sat together on the black love seat in the living room, sipping our breakfast tea. As we looked out the long expanse of windows facing the lake, we saw a great blue heron skim low over the water, like a silent phantom. We watched it glide up the length of the lake, veering left toward the northern shore before disappearing from view. When it was no longer visible, Alice turned to me and quietly informed me that herons and cranes are Chinese symbols of long life.

"Perhaps," she said softly, "this one is a messenger, an omen of good things to come for you and Ted."

"Perhaps so," I replied, as I leaned toward her, finding comfort in her embrace.

Ted's surgery is scheduled for December 10th. I hope the surgeon can completely resect this cancer and that Ted will have many more years left to live. That is my deepest hope, my dearest prayer.

Our house

Notes from the Catastrophic Realm

Our view of Lake Orange

Our backyard

A letter written to Doris, my beloved mother in law, mother of Stefan, my first husband.

November 30, 1997

Dear Doris:

I have terrible news: Ted has pancreatic cancer.

As you may know, pancreatic cancer carries a dreadful prognosis. It is fast growing and usually deadly. We are both quite shocked to have this thrust upon us. Ted comes from a long-lived and robust family. His mother died at age eighty-five and his father is alive and healthy at eighty-eight. All his grandparents lived well into their eighties, so this is quite surprising. Ted looks and feels as well as ever.

We have gotten one bit of hopeful news. The biopsy indicates he may not have the usual form of pancreatic cancer, but rather a more indolent variety which could be surgically resectable. The surgery is extensive and carries a mortality rate of five percent with a complication rate of fifty percent, but, of course, people do survive it and if we are lucky, it could be a cure. We have scheduled the surgery for December 10th at Duke Medical Center. We like the surgeon and he is very experienced at this procedure.

So that is where we are--not any place we expected to be, but such is life. Believe it or not, this has not been a total nightmare. I am learning that everything comes with its own gifts, even something as awful as this. Ted has reacted to this diagnosis with grace and equanimity. He is most concerned about me but I tell him I will be all right. I am grateful for the time we have had together and glad I can be with him on this fateful journey.

We are determined to make the best of every day until December 10th and we hope the surgery can be successfully accomplished. If it is not, we will see an oncologist to buy as much time as we can, but that is only our fall-back position. Foremost in our minds is not to lose today by being fearful about tomorrow.

Believe it or not, we had a wonderful Thanksgiving. My dear friend Alice, an accomplished and imaginative chef, flew down from New York to create a gourmet feast for us. She conjured up enough exquisite food to last a month and we had a lovely day enjoying Alice's sumptuous table and each other's company.

Everyone has been good to us. My brother Joel and his wife, Kane, have been phoning frequently, sustaining us with their concern. My beloved Aunt Sylvia will come up from Florida right after Ted's surgery. Alice returns in January after Aunt Sylvia goes home, and Ted's son, Charles and his wife, Susan, are coming from Ontario, a few days before the surgery. Karen and Kennie, Ted's sister and brother, will fly in from western Canada during Ted's recuperation, and Ted's former student, Fumiko, is coming soon from New York City. We are grateful for all this love and feel very well cared for.

I'm sorry to have to report such unhappy news, Doris, but I'm hoping we'll be lucky and that surgery will provide a happy end to this story. Please keep us in your heart and prayers.

Much love,
Judy

December 2, 1997

Ted is having a colonoscopy tomorrow and I hope there are no surprises. It's a routine pre-operative test and the doctor doesn't expect to find cancer in Ted's colon, but then he didn't expect it to turn up in his pancreas either.

I will try to have as positive an attitude as Ted. He looks at the fifty percent survival statistic the surgeon quotes and envisions a cure, while I see mortality loitering in the background like a menacing thug. Well, Ted was the happy child raised in the rugged paradise of the Canadian Rockies and embraced by a loving family. I was the skinny, sad-eyed girl, bewildered by my mother's brittle self-centeredness and inability to love me. No wonder we look at the world through a different lens.

Then, too, I've been here before. Stefan was supposed to have had a benign brain tumor, easily resected, but the surgeon was wrong and it was no such thing. It was a viper slithering through his brain. He was thirty-six when he was diagnosed with brain cancer and I was thirty. We had been married seven years. Five years later, Stefan was dead and I was a widow. So maybe I've earned the right to get jittery when surgeons pontificate and tell me they think this and that.

Even so, God's grace will surely be with us as we make our way through the valley of the shadow. It will bring us strength and keep us whole. It will help me to remember that there are bluebirds and owls, deer and roses at my doorstep, as well as cancer and fear and sorrow. It will remind me that love is not measured in increments of time but by the fullness of our hearts, and that we all live, tottering at the abyss, on borrowed time.

December 3, 1997

I met Ted at his office today since we were going to the clinic for his colonoscopy. The Canadian Studies Center at Duke University, where Ted is based as a professor of British and Canadian literature, is housed in a lovely former home on a tree-lined campus street. After climbing the back stairs leading directly to his office, I saw Ted clearly through the glass-paned door. He was seated in his brown leather chair, his feet crossed and comfortably propped up on the edge of his large oak desk. He was thoroughly engrossed in a Canadian literary journal. For a moment, I simply stood at the door and watched him, enjoying the concentration and pleasure so evident on his face. Then I brought my attention back to the task at hand, knocked on the door, turned its knob and walked in. Ted looked up and a smile bloomed on his face; rising from his chair, he enfolded me in a hug, planting a kiss in my hair.

When he sat down again, he delivered the sober news that a lesser dean had just informed him he would not get his full salary nor would any of his benefits accrue during his medical leave. He would get seventy-five percent of his salary, minus the cost of his health insurance premiums. This was to start immediately.

Previously, we had been told by his Department Chair that Ted would receive his full salary and benefits during his sick leave. Now, it seemed, we had to worry not only about a life-threatening illness, but about paying the mortgage and medical expenses, as well. I was in a fretful mood when we left for the clinic.

Once inside the clinic building, we made our way through a maze of corridors to the GI Procedures Suite. It was a cramped basement space, painted a putrid bile green. After presenting ourselves at the front desk, we sat on molded plastic chairs and waited almost two hours, surrounded by an array of people in varying states of ill health. Finally, a nurse called for Ted, apologizing for the delay, saying it was one of their more frantic days, when everything took longer than usual and back-ups increased exponentially as the day progressed. Then she gathered us up and shepherded us into the suite. After Ted was put into a hospital gown and positioned on a stretcher, the nurse threaded a catheter into a vein in his left forearm, connecting it to a bag that dripped saline solution slowly into his arm. Shortly thereafter, he was wheeled into the interior of the suite and I went off to obtain the surgeon's signature on the Family Medical Leave request I wanted to submit to my employer.

An hour later, I returned to the GI Procedure Suite, sure that Ted would be finishing up, but even after another hour passed, there was no sign of him. Neither had anyone come to tell me what was happening or why the procedure was taking so long. It was nearly the end of the day and, one by one, nurses began leaving. I needed to find someone who could give me information, so I ambushed a young male nurse heading out the door and begged him to find Ted for me. Undoubtedly sensing my impending descent into hysteria, he went back into the suite from which he had just emerged, reappearing a short time later to assure me that all was well. It seems the scope was reluctant to take some sharp turns round Ted's colon and the doctor wanted as complete an exam as possible. Once again, I was left to wait in the depressing green sitting area, but at least the images of mayhem, which had begun insinuating themselves into my consciousness, began to recede.

Eventually, Ted appeared on a gurney, exultant and smiling. Because of the doctor's persistence, Ted's colon had been completely visualized and he would be spared the additional discomfort of a barium study. Most important, the news was good: nary a polyp had been found.

From the gurney, Ted moaned dramatically that he was starving, so after the nurse removed his IV and checked his vital signs, and when he was again garbed in his own clothes, we left the clinic for *Ben and Jerry's*, where Ted devoured a double dip black cherry ice cream cone in record time.

We arrived home to find a message on our answering machine. The business manager of the Canadian Studies Center had called to tell us the lesser dean was incorrect: Ted would receive his full salary and benefits. We cheered and hugged and laughed with relief, celebrating our good fortune by sprawling across the love seat in front of the fireplace with a glass or two of plum wine.

May that fellow remain a lesser dean forever.

December 4, 1997

I see signs and portents in everything. I look for omens in cloud formations and find messages from the gods in weather patterns. I am amazed by the extent of my own superstition but I suppose it's to be expected: it's only a longing to know the unknowable, an attempt to find solace while lost in a maze made from my own fear.

I pray for Ted to do well during surgery. My deepest wish is that his cancer is operable. I want Ted to go on teaching for many years, and I want to grow old within the frame of his love. It would be too cruel for this not to happen; Ted is so deserving, and I have already witnessed one good man die too soon. Yet I can only pray and hope, and ultimately respond to whatever fate dictates.

I will confront whatever happens because that's what love is about: doing the hard stuff. Love isn't the soft-focus treacle of romantic movies or the sexual passion of erotica. It's a primal force of nature, a fierce and striving energy enabling one to act with heroic strength. I know this. It is the lesson of my life.

I learned it several years after Stefan died, while still adrift in anger and sorrow. One day, I just happened to look hard at the vibrant beauty of a single iris in a New York City flower shop. I noticed how beautiful it was, its slender green stem and soft, fragile petals, the purity of its vivid blue and the rousing vigor of its central splash of yellow. It was as if I were seeing an iris for the first time and it took my breath away. Alongside death and despair, in an unfair and capricious world, there was also this: unadulterated beauty, and it was no less abundant in the world than cancer and death and grief. I realized, in that moment, that I had been dishonoring the memory of Stefan's life by carelessly throwing my own away. On that day, I found a reason to choose life over death, and love over despair.

Notes from the Catastrophic Realm

Now, all these years later, facing a similar ordeal, I look back at that day with gratitude for all the blessings that flowed from it. Sitting in front of the crackling fireplace, sipping tea, I recall these things while my sweet kitty, Tilla, is folded into a curl in my lap, purring a contented vibrato into the listening air. Life is a complicated endeavor, I muse, not readily reducible to easy judgments.

December 8, 1997

This morning at breakfast, Ted gave me a hug and a poem that he wrote late last night. He hasn't written any poetry for me in several months. Well, he certainly has other things to think about, so it's particularly sweet to get this little gift.

The last time he wrote any of his "bad poetry," as he calls it, was last summer, after he falsely accused Tilla of dining on the koi in our fish pond. After we discovered the real culprit, a raccoon, Ted felt guilty about unjustly blaming my innocent kitty, so he wrote a little verse for me, exonerating Tilla of all responsibility for our rapidly diminishing fish population.

I love these poems that Ted writes just for me and though he'll never be a poet laureate, (and it's good he has a day job), he's one of my favorite poets for sure.

I hope I'm as strong as Ted thinks I am. Most of the time, I feel only a heartbeat away from totally falling apart, or maybe just hiding under the covers for a century or two.

Notes from the Catastrophic Realm

It's only with a real test
One has a chance to show one's best.
I'm most impressed.
She's rock-hard solid at the core,
A woman well worth living for.

We've had some years in which we two
Our life and love could both renew.
But some's too few.
I hope I might have thirty more,
With one so well worth living for.

Yet thirty years would still not be
Enough to show what she's to me.
Eternity...
Is ample time to full adore
A woman so well worth living for.

Ted Davidson
December, 1997

December 9, 1997

Ted's surgery is tomorrow. We went for his pre-operative work-up today and spent the better part of the day at the hospital. This process is not designed for the convenience of the patient; still, everyone was pleasant and if it took way too long, at least it all got done. Now there is only the interminable waiting.

I have begun to bargain with God for increments of success. Now I ask only that the tumor is operable. Then, once it's out, I'll petition for an uneventful recovery. I am hoping for this with all the hope my heart has ever held. I am wishing and pleading and praying that death will back away and amble diffidently into the distant future, leaving me to live within Ted's love for years to come.

December 10, 1997

Charles and Susan drove us to the hospital, heading east on the highway, right into a round orange sun beginning its climb at the bottom edge of the morning sky. Ted was his usual cheerful self, but the rest of us were struggling with our feelings, and the best I could do was affect a forced cheerfulness.

We parked Charles's Volkswagen in the medical center parking deck, walking across the street to the hospital's main entrance, then riding the elevator up to the third floor. After a brief stay in a nondescript waiting room, Ted's name was called and a nurse escorted us to the operating room holding area, where she took Ted's vital signs, checked him in, and assigned him to a small, private cubicle, before leaving.

Ted changed into a shapeless hospital gown and stuffed his belongings into a large plastic shopping bag. Moments later, the nurse re-appeared, helping him onto the stretcher that would soon take him into the OR, then deftly starting an IV in his forearm before leaving again. As Ted lay on the stretcher waiting, he was relaxed and curious, casually chatting with me and Charles.

I, however, was becoming more terrified by the second, though I tried to hide it by acting as if this were a perfectly ordinary experience. Yet, life had ceased to be ordinary the moment Ted's cancer was diagnosed and, maybe, I just knew too much. Fifteen years of experience as an open-heart operating room nurse had taught me how much can go wrong during surgery, and this procedure is particularly challenging, both for the surgeon and the patient.

A young woman in green scrubs approached us, introducing herself as Ted's anesthesiologist. She was startled to learn that her patient's son was a lawyer and his wife was a health care risk manager at the competing university hospital. Laughingly, she assured us she'd be extra careful to provide excellent care.

Ted reluctantly removed his wedding band at the anesthesiologist's insistence, handing it to me with instructions to slip it back on his finger as soon as he came out of surgery. He kissed Charles, and then he kissed me, and then the anesthesiologist took him away. Charles and I watched as she wheeled the gurney down a long corridor, through blue automatic double doors that opened, like the wide menacing maw of some mythical beast, into the interior of the surgical suite.

After Ted was out of sight, Charles, Susan and I returned to the parking deck to put Ted's clothes in the car. On our way out, the receptionist handed me a beeper in case she needed to reach me while we were gone. Our task took longer than anticipated because we couldn't remember where we had parked and, consequently, we walked each of the deck's five levels, more than once, before locating our car.

As we returned to the waiting room, the receptionist smiled and thanked us for answering her page. I told her that she must be mistaken, that Ted's surgery would take many more hours and we hadn't received a page.

"Oh yes," she said, " I paged you myself, at the surgeon's request. He'll be out to speak to you shortly."

My insides twisted into hard, tense knots, and my eyes filled with tears as I recognized what was occurring. It was as if I were re-living Stefan's surgery all over again, so many years later. The very same thing was happening: it wasn't what they anticipated, they couldn't get it out, they were very sorry. I hugged myself as I rocked back and forth, wondering how this could possibly be, how could Ted, vigorous and healthy, have inoperable, advanced pancreatic cancer?

Some sweet soul shepherded us to into a small private waiting room where I sat between Susan and Charles, shaking and sobbing. I felt Charles holding me tight around the waist, as though he thought I might rise out of my chair, powered only by grief, and fly clear through the hospital rooftop, shrieking and howling over the Durham streets. Susan sat on my other side, hugging me, but what I noticed most were the burning hot tears sliding down my cheeks and the shrill echo of my own mournful voice, wailing pitifully.

My heart is breaking into a thousand useless pieces. Vitality oozes from every pore and something that feels like death constricts me in its vise-like grip. I can barely breathe, though I hardly care. My jumbled mind is straining to make sense of this. Perhaps we were too happy, happier than we had a right to be? We were, indeed, so very happy, but now everything is over and nothing matters, nothing at all.

We did not deserve this, Ted and I, but then no one does. And even now, in the fulminating presence of horror, the deepest, sanest part of me knows that God is not punishing my happiness, and a voice deep inside my head reminds me that this is nothing other than life coming round to collect its due, for we all owe life a death.

But I cannot bear it, I cannot.

Thursday, December 17, 1997

Everything has changed since Ted's surgery. I feel as if time has stopped and life itself has paused, taking a sharp turn around a cruel corner to become something else entirely, something that suddenly seems dangerous. I am afraid of every possibility now, and I notice how gossamer the veil is that separates life from death.

Yet, Ted's recovery is progressing well. On this sunlit winter day, we walked a mile together, fetching our mail from the mailbox at the end of our road. It was an accomplishment for Ted, a testimony to his increasing strength. I've been retrieving the mail alone this past week, missing his company on my solitary walks, so today was a joy, making me almost believe we could reclaim the sweet life we lived before cancer intruded, but, of course, that cannot be. Life has changed irrevocably for both of us and nothing will be as it once was. Our innocence is gone and the honeymoon is certainly over.

After getting the mail, we drove into town and ate lunch at *The Saratoga Grill*. It was such an ordinary pleasure: sitting at a neighborhood restaurant having lunch with my husband. Yet, in the context of our new lives, it wasn't ordinary at all, and my appetite increased with the realization that Ted is stronger each day.

After lunch, we drove to the farm where I board my quarter horse, Lucky. It had been over two weeks since we had last seen or ridden him, longer than usual. We spotted him at the far end of the largest paddock, lazily swishing his luxurious, white tail as he and two companions grazed on flakes of hay. Ted gave a yell and Lucky, raising his beautiful gray head, whinnied a greeting in return and then flew toward us at a gallop, holding his tail high, like an unfurled banner, until he stopped short, just inches in front of us, bits of hay still clinging to his upper lip. We buried our hands in the soft warmth of his dense winter coat, offering carrots and stroking his ears, while he nickered and nuzzled and rubbed his big head on our jackets. I breathed softly into his nostrils and then, with Ted's help, clambered onto his back, gripping his broad sides with my legs as I grabbed a hank of mane, before sending him off on a cadenced canter around the perimeter of the paddock. As I sat to the rocking rhythm of his gait, feeling the power and warmth of his muscles and the elasticity of his spine beneath me, I felt capable and happy for the first time since Ted's surgery. Anxiety melted away as Lucky and I made figure eights across the paddock, while Ted, hands thrust into his jacket pockets, looking healthy and hale, stood in the grass smiling, watching us with obvious pleasure.

Eventually, we jogged over to Ted, who grabbed hold of Lucky's halter, while I slid off his side. Ted clipped a lead-line to the halter, and I held it, while he vigorously cleaned out Lucky's feet with a pick. Then we brushed his long winter coat, gave him another carrot or two, undid the lead-line, and waved him off to rejoin his friends, while we walked, hand in hand, back to the car. It was a good day; I hope for more.

Lucky and I

December 21, 1997

My old life with Ted is over, I have a new one now, not the life I wanted or expected, but it's the one I've been given and I need to adapt. Death resides at its farthest limit and its foremost characteristic is the body's blithe betrayal as it responds to a clamor for cell growth, more insistent than life itself.

Yesterday, we met with the oncologist, Dr. M, who determined that Ted's chemotherapy would begin in about two weeks. We are hopeful Ted will experience a significant remission from this chemotherapy but we are also aware there is no cure. The aborted surgery dispelled that hope. Now we speak only in terms of small increments of time, bought with the help of toxic drugs; now I think in terms of months and seasons, not years.

Yet Ted and I still have smiles for one another and outside there is the spare beauty of green pines and tall skeletal oaks shimmering in a golden wash of pale winter sunlight. These are the things that sustain me, but just barely.

Christmas Eve, 1997

Charles wanted a Christmas tree. Ted, Susan and I were indifferent, but Charles really wanted it, so he and I ran out on Christmas Eve day to bring one home. We thought we might drive to Susan and Alex's farm, where Lucky lives, and having received their permission, cut a tree from their woods, but the day was cold and rainy, not the sort of weather to be tramping through acreage chopping down a tree.

Instead we went to a local tree lot and found a small fragrant spruce. We secured it to the car and then drove off in search of a Christmas tree stand, since ours had apparently gone missing. *Walmart*, we soon discovered, had sold out and so had the garden shop near home. A fellow there suggested a shop on St. Mary's Road, so we hopped back in the car, heading off in the direction we had just come from. By the time we arrived at our destination, it was raining hard and the shop was closed, but an assortment of lawn ornaments were scattered about the front yard. Charles and I poked around in the downpour, sloshing through viscous mud without encountering even one Christmas tree stand, but we did spot a cement planter we thought would do. It cost twenty-four dollars. We lugged it to the car and heaved it into the trunk, vowing to return with money after the holiday. Then we sped home through the rain, congratulating ourselves on our inventiveness.

At an informal family meeting, we decided to set the tree in the living room, near the glass doors that open to the garden path leading down to the lake. Charles and Susan maneuvered the tree into the planter, carefully wedging it firmly in place with spare pieces of lumber. Then Charles filled it with water and draped a festive red tablecloth around the whole thing. Ted soon noticed that it was leaking all over the floor (all of us having conveniently forgotten that cement is porous) but the problem was quickly solved by hoisting the soggy mess into a large green plastic laundry basket.

Once that crisis was resolved, we got busy: hanging ornaments, flinging tinsel over boughs, looping strings of white lights across branches, laughing and joking and enjoying the zesty scent of pine, as we dressed our tree in sparkles and light. By the time we finished and I had carefully set our starched, white, hand-crocheted angel at the very top, and placed our gifts beneath, it was almost dark. We gave Ted the honor of flipping the switch to light the tree. As he flicked it on, our modest spruce was transformed into a luminous confection, spilling color, light and cheer into every corner of the room. We stood before it transfixed, mouths agape, eyes wide, staring like children at the beautiful thing we had created.

It's always a treat to see an evergreen twinkling with light in bleak December, but this year, when we are so somber and anxious, this small, splendid tree is a true beacon of hope.

Charles was right, we needed a Christmas tree, more than we realized.

December 28, 1997

It's Monday, the beginning of a new week, and Ted and I have decided to tackle some of the chores we've neglected of late. We need to go to the bank, we have letters to mail and garbage to take to the dump. We also want to shop for a new car. Life goes on.

But upon leaving our local bank this afternoon, Ted complained of stomach cramps and said he would rather go home and rest than drive into Chapel Hill to buy a car. So Charles, who was driving, turned the car around and we headed for home.

As we crept through a Hillsborough traffic snarl, snow began falling, and soon large fluffy flakes blanketed the ground in chaste white. Our car crawled silently along, while large, delicate snowflakes clung to the windshield or melted on the windows, and snow swirled everywhere, turning the world white, as we continued our drive north. Soon, everything around us looked different, altered, as if by magic, to resemble a winter landscape sketched by *Currier and Ives*. As we turned onto Arrowhead Trail and pulled into our driveway, we three were changed too. Ted's cramps had abated and we were enchanted by the seasonal beauty that had come on so suddenly, unexpectedly enfolding everything in glistening white brightness.

We climbed out of the car and decided to walk down the hill behind the house to look at the lake. Charles walked ahead, Ted and I following behind. Ours were the first footprints in the snow, except for a deer or two that had already paid their respects. The lake was tranquil and opaque; the sky was the color of slate. Snow clung lightly to spindly pine branches and traced the leafless shapes of oaks. It was very beautiful and very quiet. It felt as if we were standing in a large, majestic cathedral and perhaps, in the truest sense, we were. I stood silently next to Ted, breathing in the hushed beauty of my own backyard and, for a moment, I was transported beyond time or understanding, to a liminal state of grace.

Then a sudden sharp wind, whipping across my cheek, made me shiver, and Ted put his arm around my shoulders, suggesting we walk home, make a fire in the fireplace, and shake off our chill with a glass of plum wine. It seemed a good idea, so shouting out our intentions to Charles, we turned and trudged back up the snowy hill, passing the breeze way and our newly frozen koi pond, before reaching the inviting warmth beckoning at our front door.

December 29, 1997

Dear John,

We didn't send out cards this year because shortly before Christmas I received some bad news. In late November, I found out I had pancreatic cancer. At first it looked operable, but when that was tried the surgeon found that the cancer had spread. So in a couple of weeks as soon as I am more fully recovered from the surgery, I will start chemotherapy and we'll see what can be done on that front.

All in all, I'm in pretty good shape both physically and emotionally. I bounced back from the surgery and in other ways, too. I'm not letting the disease keep me down. My son and daughter-in-law are here for the holidays and we had a great Christmas. Judy, my wife, is being wonderfully supportive. I plan to teach next term (I still much enjoy working with Duke students) and to continue, as much as possible, my normal life. Life is a gift, after all, and none of us know for how long we may have it.

On a different note, congratulations on re-reading all of Trollope. I am impressed and am tempted to partial emulation. Perhaps all of Conrad. But more likely, all of Margaret Atwood, for I am teaching a course on her fiction next term. And still on the subject of reading, are you familiar with the fiction of James Welch, Louise Erdrich, and Thomas King? Most of my students find Welch's *Fool's Crow*, and Erdrich's *Tracks* to be particularly rewarding, and the all-time favorite in the course in which I teach it is King's *Green Grass, Running Water*. Let me know what you think of especially that last one.

Looking forward to hearing from you further. And best wishes for a rewarding new year.

As ever,

Ted

December 31, 1997

Charles, Susan and I are downstairs in the kitchen preparing a venison feast for our New Year's Eve dinner tonight. Charles and Susan will return home to Canada this week-end, and Ted and I will surely miss them. This visit has been good for all of us and I've especially enjoyed watching Ted and Charles together. They execute a poetic body language, folding constantly towards one another, braiding themselves around each other in graceful postures of devotion, yet they are entirely unaware that they are engaged in such a tender pas de deux.

Charles has repaired numerous household appliances since he's been here. He's unclogged drains and calmed jittery toilets. He's done yard work, flipped mattresses and unstuck windows. And each evening we congregate in the living room, while he plays the shakohatchi, his Japanese flute, and Ted, sitting near the fire, meditates, eyes closed, breath regular, visualizing the death of cancer cells. The shakohatchi has a more plaintive sound than the western flute; complex and rich, it conveys depths of emotions I can barely express in words. It sounds of experience, with top notes of melancholy, invigorated by a deep vibrant tone. It's a lovely, haunting sound, and both Ted and I find these evening meditations restorative.

There is something to be said for living intentionally---for understanding in every cell of one's being that this is all a gift---each day, each hour, each precious parcel of time. Neither life nor love is promised to any of us, and to have experienced both is perhaps an unmerited blessing.

I don't know how long Ted will live. I had hoped we would grow old together, had assumed we would have at least twenty years before death came for one of us, but we will not be so lucky. I weep for lost possibilities and unrealized hopes but I also recognize that Ted and I have a bond that can transcend even death. He will remain in my heart until death takes me too, reuniting us deep in the earth or high in the night sky as the formative stuff of new life. It has always been so and so it will always be.

January 1, 1998

It's the first day of the new year and I'm afraid to consider too closely what it may hold for me and Ted. I wonder if Ted will still be here when it ends and how much time we have left together. It looks to be an ominous and fearful year, yet Ted is hopeful. He thinks it will be a good year and maybe he is right. We are not doing too badly. Ted is recovering quickly from his aborted surgery and we are learning to live within uncertainty, even while death lounges nearby. We are getting better at gratitude, recognizing the immense gift of love flowing to us from friends and family. We better appreciate the sight and touch of each other. These are not bad things.

We finally bought a new car yesterday. We looked at a Mitsubishi Galant and a Toyota Camry but ended up with a Honda Accord. We could have gotten a discount if we had purchased the white model we test drove around Chapel Hill, but Ted spied a silver-blue color he liked better, so that's the one we bought.

When we first decided to buy a car, the plan was that Ted would use my car and I would drive the new one, but it's working out differently. Ted likes this silvery car so much that it seems he should have it, and I would be dishonest if I denied that, in the back of my mind, is the sad thought that this will be his last car, so I want him to enjoy it. Besides, it goes nicely with his blue eyes.

January 6, 1998

I'm concerned that Ted isn't eating enough. He's been nauseated for the past two days and has lost weight since his surgery. He now weighs 155 pounds, substantially less than his usual 180 pound self. I worry that he likes his new svelte shape; after all, he's spent much of his adult life watching his weight and now he's finally slim, but I fear he will continue losing weight once his chemotherapy begins.

He did have a productive day, though. This morning he made a dump run to the landfill, then chatted with numerous friends and neighbors, and later yet, he asked me to type ten pages of his memoir, *Mountain Views,* about growing up on a cattle ranch in rural Alberta. He also confirmed that he will teach an undergraduate course on Margaret Atwood's fiction this spring, as he had planned to do before cancer so rudely intruded on our lives. He has thirty students registered, with a waiting list of twenty more. It will be good medicine for him to be back in a classroom again.

I had an interesting day, too. It was my first day back at work since Ted's surgery and recollections of life prior to Ted's cancer flooded my mind with sadness and longing, as I realized how innocently I had lived that life, never imagining any other possibility. Still, it was lovely to see Mareid, Denise, and Sally, my colleagues at the UNC Hospital Risk Management Department. They have been immeasurably kind, supporting me throughout this ordeal, and being back among them was just as enjoyable as plunging into work that provides me with a sense of normalcy and routine.

But I do find myself surreptitiously watching everyone at work as they go about their ordinary lives. I notice how often they become caught up in the small, inconsequential dramas that epitomize daily existence and I recognize that I, too, used to do the same thing. It's interesting to keep in mind that "normal life" is made up of just these things, daily dramas and routine chores that need to be reckoned with, as we put one foot in front of the other, traversing each day with determination and attention, never considering the possibility that we might, on this very day, or any given moment, cross paths with calamity or be snared in a trap laid by our own fragile mortality. How sweetly innocent my dear co-workers seem, oblivious to the precarious nature of ordinary life and how easily one may tumble out of it into this parallel universe of cataclysmic illness.

January 9, 1998

Ted started his chemotherapy yesterday. It will drip into his vein over several hours every Thursday for the next seven weeks, after which he will undergo an MRI to evaluate its effect. I'm glad it has finally started because he seems more symptomatic than he was a month ago---more pain, more nausea, more fatigue. I'm concerned the tumor may be growing faster than we thought. I hope I'm wrong about this, perhaps these symptoms are merely a response to the assault of surgery and not an indication of advancing disease, but I can't quiet my suspicions.

There is also a new and disturbing difference in Ted's emotional state. He had anticipated, thoroughly believed, there would be a surgical cure. It's been hard for him to relinquish that possibility, harder yet to confront the unadorned prospect of death this illness presents. How could he not be depressed and frightened by the road ahead? Nevertheless, it's vital that he not become lost to self-pity or fear. The only way out of despair is to plow through it and I know Ted can do this, but he needs to be aware that he's falling into a dangerous state of passivity.

Consequently, tonight while we were sitting on the love seat by the fireplace sipping plum wine, I initiated a conversation about the importance of being proactive. I told Ted that he must find a way to marshal the energy to defend his own life, to will himself to eat despite nausea and to live as fully as he is able. If he succumbs to the temptations of depression and fear they will prove deadly because hope and joy are as vital as courage. It was a good dialogue and I'm glad we talked of these things openly. Ted acknowledged that, of late, he feels caught in a web of fear and sadness that is immobilizing him, and he's decided to schedule an appointment

A Love Story

with a psychologist he likes, who, years ago, helped him through divorce.

Our discussion brought to mind one of my favorite sayings of Rabbi Nachman of Bratslav,[1] which was turned into a popular Israeli song decades ago by the late singer and rabbi, Shlomo Carlbach. Emboldened by two or three (or four?) glasses of plum wine, I sang it for Ted. He loved it, so I taught him the words and then we sang it together, whole rousing choruses, all the while interspersing our singing with a few more splashes of plum wine, until suddenly I began crying and Ted, reaching over to comfort me, began to cry too. We held each other tightly, crying until we had no tears left, and then we started singing again, softly at first, then louder and louder, as we were grabbed by the melody and empowered words, or the wine, or the determined dissonance of our own off-key voices. We finally tired ourselves out singing triumphantly (and drinking less triumphantly), so staggering from the love seat, we tottered toward the staircase, hanging onto each other and the banister as we lurched up the stairs to our bedroom, crashing with a thud onto our big iron bed, hoping for dreams of good times yet to be.

---

1 *Kol ha'olam kulo gesher tzar m'ode, ve'ha'ikar lo lefached k'lal.*
   The whole world is a very narrow bridge and the main thing is not to be afraid at all.
   Rabbi Nachman of Bratslav, 19th. Century Chasidic Rabbi

January 21, 1998

Ted had his third chemotherapy treatment today. It's beginning to seem almost natural to go to the clinic, stay there six hours while Ted has blood tests, sees the oncologist, and finally gets hooked up to an IV for his weekly dose of Gemcitabine.

It's been about two months since we learned of this cancer and the initial shock is gone. Now there are times I can almost forget there's a tumor nestled coyly in Ted's belly, now life goes on despite cancer. We are both back at work and grateful to be there.

Ted has been using very little pain medication this week. I like to think it's an indication that the chemotherapy is working but I'm not sure that's really true. It might only be that he's healed from the surgery since his pain level prior to the aborted operation was minimal. So perhaps there is no change, perhaps this chemo is doing nothing at all.

There are four more treatments left so, for the next little while, I can go on believing that good things are happening, that this chemo is slaying cancer cells galore, that we will prevail, and that Ted will survive indefinitely, happy and hale, on relatively benign chemotherapeutic cocktails.

February 1, 1998

My Aunt Sylvia visited us from Florida and she was as full of beans as ever. Her generosity of spirit and the joyful way she lives, with exaltation and exuberance shining in her eyes, has inspired and delighted me since childhood. My auntie has consistently been the person I could count on for anything, especially love, which she possesses in abundance and gives away freely. As I grew to maturity, I recognized the sterling example she set before me of how one might live life with gratitude for the good and a graceful valiant resilience for the harder times. Simply being in her presence is both a joy and a lesson and this visit was no different, only perhaps more necessary, hence even more appreciated.

We had such fun together, despite her and Ted's stubborn determination to watch every moment of every Duke basketball game on TV. Even so, she still found time for long, intimate chats with me, often continuing into the early hours of morning and always accompanied by her sublime home-baked Linzer tarts and hot tea.

Aunt Sylvia fed me and Ted like the Jewish (grand) mother she is, presenting more platters and bowls of delicious, aromatic food at each meal than twenty people could consume, baking dozens of sugar-dusted Linzer tarts and assorted varieties of rugelach, and then constantly urging us to eat more, more, more. It was easy to accommodate her, even Ted hardly stopped eating and actually gained a couple of pounds, and if anyone could simply love Ted back into good health, it would be my auntie. When she left to return home, our house felt like a fierce but loving whirlwind had swept through it, fumigating our fears, purifying our hearts, scrubbing and polishing our resolve, leaving in its wake the refreshing, strengthening, scent of 100% pure love.

A day after Aunt Sylvia went home, Karen and Kennie, Ted's sister and brother, arrived. Karen came from Calgary; Kennie flew here from Vancouver. The three of them stayed up late, night after night, reminiscing about growing up on the family ranch, just outside the small village of Mountain View, Alberta. I was enchanted by the wholesome exuberance of their exploits, and listened intently, experiencing the occasional twinge of envy. They seem so grounded in their sense of family and place, having grown up on land homesteaded by their family several generations back. To me, a childhood like theirs, spent among the companionship of ranch dogs, barn cats and horses, rounding up cattle each summer with their dad, and being tended to and loved by a large, extended family, seems nothing less than idyllic.

Now Karen and Kennie have also gone home, and Ted and I are alone for the first time in weeks. This afternoon, we took a walk along Arrowhead Trail, before turning onto the path that leads to the bright red barn and its adjacent pasture at the end of the trail. Two horses live there, a chestnut and a bay, but neither were present today. Perhaps, on this mild sunny afternoon they were out being ridden, but we were disappointed, missing the soft nickers and whinnies our arrival usually elicited.

Ted has three more chemotherapy treatments left. I'm hoping he will have a good response to this drug, but I'm jittery and anxious and need to stop concocting imaginary worst-case scenarios in my head. It does no good to scare myself by daydreaming about every dreadful possibility. I'd be wiser to concentrate my energy on enjoying every sweet morsel of life: right here, right now.

I noticed yesterday that the birds have discovered the feeders I hung for them. Now, when we look toward the lake from the living room, or the kitchen, or the breakfast nook, we see wrens, finches, and cardinals congregating at the bird feeders like workers gathering and gossiping around the office coffee pot. I'm pleased to make their winter a little easier, and in return Ted and I get to enjoy their considerable charm. It seems a fair exchange.

February 5, 1998

It's Thursday again, and soon we will leave for Duke's Cancer Clinic and another chemotherapy treatment. It's not my favorite day. This is the most obvious reminder that we are precariously balanced, poised tenuously between life and death. Of course, now I live with a heightened awareness of death's possibility. I recognize its shadow lurking in Ted's appearance, in my own anxiety, in the way tears pool just behind my eyes, ready to fall. Yet going to the hospital each week and watching a young, coltish nurse thread an IV needle into Ted's arm is the worst reminder of this reality. I try to tell myself that this is helping him, that it is allowing me to keep him close longer, but I am not so sure. I know this disease. It is brutal, savage, and as aggressive as a charging bull. It is relentless, without mercy, and there is no cure.

I try to take all of Ted into my brain, like communion, I ingest him body and blood, heart and soul, keeping the feel of his skin on my skin, memorizing his grin and learning by heart the safety that washes over me when his large hand clasps my own. I do this consciously, so I can keep him alive, in my life, for the rest of my years.

February 12, 1998

I spent this morning dusting, vacuuming, and watching the birds at their feeders. Ted has been reading an Atwood novel since breakfast in preparation for Monday's class. It's another wet, wintry day. The sun has been gone for two full days now and shows no sign of returning, and yet, just this morning, Ted pointed out our first daffodil. It's in the backyard, beyond the large tree stump, huddling next to a bare-limbed oak, looking forlorn and beleaguered in the gusty wind and rain. Its dear yellow head is bowed and its fragility makes me worry for its survival, but there it is, determined and hanging on. It gives me hope and I feel a kindred relationship to it, just now.

I am looking forward to a quiet weekend with Ted and hope he doesn't have an unduly bad reaction to his chemotherapy later today. I'm hoping he will feel like himself this weekend, instead of his recently acquired, post-chemo alter-ego: the exhausted, nauseated, and perennially depleted "Fred." It's impossible to predict how the chemotherapy will affect him each week, though I'm told the side effects can be cumulative, so I hope "Fred" doesn't put in an appearance. This is treatment number five, with two more to go. I pray to God, to Jesus, to Allah, and to all the lost saints who ever were, that this stuff is working.

Love and Life/Love and Death

*A Valentine's Day Sermon by Judith Harrow
(with considerable help from Ted Davidson)*

Think of the most saccharine St. Valentine's Day card that you've ever received. Maybe it went something like this:

*Love is warm puppies
Or kittens at play
Love is the sweet kiss
I send you today.*

Somebody read that verse and found it good. Somebody paid hard-earned money for it because, at least in part, it expressed the sender's sentiments and you can only half question their taste because, after all, it was bought to be sent to you. Besides, it's true, or at least the first two lines are true. Love is warm puppies and kittens at play. Love is roses red and violets blue. Love is anything and everything alive and beautiful, an embodiment of the promise and mystery of life. The sunrise is brighter shared with someone you love, the dinner is tastier, the sex more fulfilling. We are simply more alive when we are in love and that fact gives validity to all the frilly cliches of romantic love that permeate our society and are particularly evident on Valentine's Day. So, whatever cards you got yesterday, read them carefully, recognize their truth and treasure them.

But love is also something more profound and far more complex. It is, I think, an empowering force, like steam or electricity, and for me the measure of love is the way it bears all things, even unto death. One of the most moving love poems I've ever read was written by a 17th century man, Henry King, as a tribute to his dead young wife. It concludes with the following two stanzas:

But hark! My pulse like a soft drum
Beats my approach, tells thee I come
And slow howe'er my march may be
I shall at last lie down by thee

The thought of this bids me go on,
And wait my dissolution
With hope and comfort. Dear (forgive
the crime) I am content to live
Divided, with but half a heart,
Til we shall meet and never part.

The truth is, love and death are related. It's uncomfortable, but they go together like the proverbial hand and glove, like love and marriage. My former UU minister in NYC, Forrest Church, son of the late US Senator, Frank Church, had a lot to say about love and death. I'd like to share some of his thoughts with you.

Forrest says,

"Love and death go together. Some people protect themselves from death by avoiding love. They have a point, for without love there is so much less to lose. You may be one of those who resist love because you know this. You know that the more you care, the more you give your life and your heart to another, the more vulnerable you become. And you are right. The word vulnerable means precisely that: susceptible to being wounded. But here's the thing: if you don't give your heart away, it shrinks. It gets smaller and harder, smaller and harder. And then you are finally safe from loss, from loss and love, as well."

And Forrest also says this:

"I gave my heart away to my best friend in college and he broke it when he died of pneumonia at the age of nineteen. I gave my heart to my father who broke it when he died of cancer at age fifty-nine. I keep giving my heart away but every time it is broken, the most amazing thing is this: it grows stronger. Not tougher, but stronger. Not more resistant to the inevitable pain that love and death bring, but more full and able to love and lose and love and lose and love and lose again."

"Love and death. Without death, love would be nothing, cheap and easy, a way to pleasure ourselves. As it is, love, however comforting, is a high-wire act. One day he will fall, or she will fall, or you will fall and there will be no net. Then cry your heart out as long as you must, but as you cry be sure to thank God. Thank God for caring so deeply that you can't bear to lose someone you love. Feel your pain and give thanks for it. For the more pain you dare to feel, the more you risk for love, the more fully alive you are." So says Forrest.

By linking love and death we come a far distance from lacey Valentines and florid proclamations of passion, far from warm puppies and heart-shaped boxes of chocolates. Yet, only a moment's reflection convinces us that Valentines Day passes and passion passes and even puppies and kittens grow up and die. What doesn't die is love. Love that has been painstakingly stitched into the fabric of a well-lived life. Love that believes all things, endures all things, hopes all things. It is only when we live fully and deeply, going to the very edge of the abyss and risking ourselves and our hearts that we do honor to the astonishing gift of life. So step out on a limb and give your heart away. I recommend it. It will be the best and the hardest thing you ever do. It may not last forever, it may sometimes make you cry, but if you accept life's dare to live without a net, in the end you will find that love, despite all its intrinsic pain and difficulty, will burnish your life to the richest gold and make it most worth living.

February 20, 1998

Ted had his last chemotherapy treatment yesterday and next week he will have an MRI to evaluate its efficacy. If it has been effective, he will begin another seven week course; if not, I don't know what we'll do, but Gemcitabine is the current drug of choice for pancreatic cancer, and if that doesn't work, others aren't likely to be more successful.

Charles and Susan are here again. Charles closed his law office for the week and the university where Susan teaches English is on winter break, so they drove down from Ontario with their new dog, Desi and arrived yesterday. Desi is a four year old, fawn colored bullmastiff, as big as a refrigerator. She looks like a boxer on steroids and would cause any intruder to think more than twice before crossing their threshold. She is a sweet, smart, formidable giant, contentedly drooling all over our wood floors, eager for treats, pats on the head, and walks by the lake. Ted and I considered getting our own bullmastiff pup (Karen, Ted's sister, owns Digger, a 160 pound bullmastiff that makes Desi look dainty) but he wasn't wild about the idea. When pressed for his feelings, he said he prefers waiting until we know the results of the MRI before we make a decision. This seems reasonable and I'm moved beyond words by his constant concern for me.

"I don't want to be gruesome," Ted told me, "but I want you to have a dog if my prognosis is poor. It will help you to have something to love, something alive and comforting, and it would make me feel better if you, at least, had that if I get sicker."

I love being loved so. I love him with all my heart for the generosity of his heart.

February 23, 1998

Night has always scared me and never more than now. My night terror is a ferocious fear of nothingness, of empty oblivion, of darkness beyond death. When all is said and done, I think my fear of the night is essentially a lack of faith.

Ted doesn't share this fear. Night comes to him as a friend, wrapping him in the soft plush of darkness, cloaking him in the beauty of stars and the serenity of planets.

I need to understand that the darkness will not hurt me. I can light up the night with candles and lamps if I desire, or better yet, I could walk outside at midnight, warmly dressed in my down parka and gray mittens. I could stroll beyond the driveway, down to Arrowhead Trail. My eyes would acclimate quickly to the darkness, and I would see the outline of bare trees along the perimeter of the pasture on the other side of the road, their silhouettes tall and straight, flattened against the blue-black sky, while high above, over everything, stretches the sheltering canopy of twinkling stars.

Stars that no longer exist still light up our night sky. The stars do their best to explain that what we think we see may not always be present, and what we don't see shouldn't necessarily be discounted. The universe, they seem to say, is replete with mystery. Make peace with it, trust its intrinsic rightness, relinquish fear.

February 25, 1998

Tomorrow we find out if this chemotherapy has done Ted any good. I'm hoping, of course, that the news will be encouraging. I think he's due some measure of good luck.

Ted received a fax at work today from his Japanese friend Hiroaki, inviting him to be the keynote speaker at a conference in Osaka next September. They will pay all his expenses plus a small honorarium. He has hoped for this to happen for several years, and he phoned me at work to tell me about the invitation, speaking with unconcealed excitement. How sweet it was to hear such happiness in his voice.

"Of course I want to go," he said. "Certainly I'll accept."

I listened on the other end of the phone, smiling at his joy while silently praying he'll still be alive next September.

February 26, 1998

The news is bad, the tumor has grown.

We left the house at noon yesterday, after walking down to the edge of the woods to see the daffodils and crocuses. There were purple, yellow and white crocuses and more than several clusters of cheerful daffodils flowering back there. Spring is definitely on its way and it's most welcome after a gray, gloomy winter.

Ted wanted to eat lunch at *The Blue Corn Cafe* before going to the hospital to see Dr. M. I was almost too nervous to eat, but Ted had a hearty appetite, even insisting on an ice-cream cone for dessert from the gelato shop next door.

We arrived at the oncology clinic on time and, as always, proceeded to wait. Ted eventually went through the usual routine of getting weighed and having his blood drawn, but we didn't see Dr. M until almost 6pm, though our appointment was at 2:30pm. There is something essentially inhumane about the whole unpleasant ordeal: the interminable waiting, the depersonalization of care, the factory-like atmosphere. It's dehumanizing for all involved, patients and practitioners alike, but there is no alternative, so one simply learns to adjust.

Dr. M was frank. The chemotherapy had not helped, the cancer had grown. He was very sorry and had hoped for a better outcome. Ted received the news with his customary grace, while I fought for composure, tears pooling just inside my eyes.

They will try another chemotherapeutic agent starting next week. The side effects will not be egregious and shouldn't prevent Ted from continuing to work. It will be given on the same schedule, an IV infusion every Thursday, and as with Gemcitabine there is no guarantee it will help, only a dash of possibility.

The only time anyone allowed us to express our feelings, indeed, even asked about our feelings, was when Rita, a young, skilled chemotherapy nurse approached me while Ted was having yet more blood drawn, following our discussion with Dr. M. With concern written large across her face, Rita said how sorry she was to have heard our bad news, then sweeping me into her arms she held me tightly. Tears began to slowly roll down my face, and soon I was sobbing relentlessly. Rita didn't shrink from my sadness, nor did it frighten her, and the comfort she imparted, merely by hugging me in silence, was a lifeline. Through that simple, generous act, she gave me a share of her own vitality, and I will remember forever the sweet release of weeping within the shelter of her embrace.

It was a relief to arrive home with Ted. We sat down together at the dining room table to discuss what this news means, and I cried a little more. Later that evening, Ted phoned Charles, who offered to fly down to be with us, then I phoned all the others who had left encouraging phone messages throughout the day, hoping to hear better news. It had been a long day and I was glad to go to bed, grateful for sleep's narcosis.

February 27, 1998

I have the opportunity to be with the person I love most in the world and share his greatest challenge. It's not what either of us would have chosen, but it's what we've been given.

Ted's response to this deadly cancer has been phenomenal. He has an understanding of life that surpasses my own and a faith in the rightness of the universe that shames my thinner faith. After a brief bout of depression, which resolved quickly with a psychologist's help, he regained his equilibrium and has never since descended into self-pity nor shrunk from the reality of death. He knows peace at his core. His concerns are mostly for Charles and me. I am learning how to die from him, and I am certainly learning how to live.

March 1, 1998

I was still reeling from the oncologist's news, feeling trapped inside a bad dream, when Ted appeared in the doorway of my study this morning. Sprawled on my green recliner, wearing a disheveled silk robe and nursing a large mug of coffee, I diffidently gazed out the window at the lake's enviable placidity, as Ted informed me that he had written a poem for me last night. He was hesitant to give it to me, he said, because he wasn't sure if it would make me feel better or worse.

"Oh," I replied flippantly, "don't worry about that. There's nothing that could possibly make me feel worse, so you might as well give it to me."

With that, he turned on his heels and I heard him rummaging in his study, before returning with a folded piece of white paper, clasped in his right hand. He offered it to me without a word and left again, obviously wanting to get out of the room before I read it.

Failing to imagine what kind of poem he could possibly have thought appropriate on this depressing occasion, I unfolded the paper and saw a short verse. I read it, then I read it again, several times.

This man, who has just found out he is dying, spent the better part of last night composing a verse to make me feel better, to help me through this ordeal, to comfort and console me. I read the poem yet again, tucking it into the heart of my heart, where, like a caterpillar that morphs into a butterfly, it changed from words on a page, into a mantra, a prayer, a hope, the distilled essence of love itself.

A Love Story

For Judy,

If I go first 'tis but to see
Just what it is that waits for thee,
And how the two of us will be
Together for Eternity.

So do not mourn when I am gone.
Our separation won't be long.
Death is just another dawn,
A different way that Life goes on.

Ted Davidson
3-2-98

March 4, 1998

Dear Charles and Susan,

    I'm sending this article that appeared in today's NY Times. It's quite coincidental because, as I mentioned to Susan in an e-message this morning, I had just called our local hospice to get information on the services they provide, how one goes about enlisting their services, and at what point it would be reasonable and advantageous to do so. I hope we are not yet at that point, but it is important to me that Ted not suffer from the inability of American medical care to deal responsibly with the process of dying. While I want to do everything possible to keep Ted happily alive for as long as possible, I also want to be mindful that care and comfort are priorities. If and when it becomes apparent that high-tech medical care in a major academic medical center is not serving Ted well, I want to be able to offer him something that will. If we are obliged to accept Ted's death, I want that death to be as gentle and sweet as possible. I don't want him in a wretched hospital room hooked up to all the gadgets in the medical armamentarium. It would serve no good end, and it's an isolated, lonely, frightening way to die. Of course, if Ted decides he wants that, so be it, but I think he has a right to know there is an alternative.

    Please let me know how you feel. I need to know. I hate to be writing this, Charles, it is so horrible to think about, but we must speak of these things and understand the implications of our decisions. Right now, I think starting the new chemotherapy is the right decision. I hope it will be what Ted needs, but if it isn't, we may need to re-think the value of putting Ted through yet another chemotherapeutic agent. I'm hoping we can trust Dr. M to be candid if he thinks we are engaged in a futile effort. I'm afraid I've seen an abrupt decline in Ted's condition this week. He's lost four pounds and feels weaker. He just seems less robust. He notices it, too. I am exceedingly grateful that he is not having more pain. He feels reasonably well and claims to be eminently able to maintain his teaching schedule, so maybe I'm being too pessimistic. I sure hope so.

I'll keep you posted about any new developments. Oh Charles, the one thing that is truly amazing is Ted's emotional state. I don't know how to describe it exactly. He is so balanced and at ease with all that is happening to him. He is not frightened by it, nor is he bitter or angry. He has not once indulged in self-pity. He wishes, of course, that this had not happened, that this experience remained far, far in his future, but as he says, one doesn't have the luxury of choice in these matters. He is pleased with the way his life has turned out and grateful for the gift of it. In the most fundamental and important ways, he truly feels he has been a lucky man. It is a privilege to witness his steadfastness and grace.

With much love,
Judy

March 7, 1998

Ted is getting sicker. The tumor is affecting his blood sugar, which is now way too high. The doctor is trying to regulate it with oral medication but it's not having much of an effect. On Monday, he will have another blood sugar level drawn, and Dr. M will either increase the dose again or prescribe a different medication. Ted has also developed trouble swallowing and a slight but persistent cough, which makes eating difficult. He's making a valiant effort to eat but it's difficult when each mouthful initiates a coughing spell and the sensation that choking is imminent. I'm so worried, so concerned, and I am bone weary.

Yet, despite all of this, Ted's spirit remains intact. He isn't undone by this betrayal of his body, indeed, I'm not sure he'd even characterize it as a betrayal. When he first learned he had cancer, Ted remarked that it was as though his cells had opted for liberation, choosing anarchy over the tedious regimentation foisted upon them by a commitment to Ted's well-being. Now they were free to do as they chose. He assumed they were having a marvelous time, behaving like raucous teenagers.

My friend Martine came by this afternoon. I hadn't seen her in ages, partially because of Ted's illness but mostly because she's been busy buying a house and moving into it. It's wonderful to see her again. We chatted with Ted for a while, but soon he went off to watch a Duke basketball game on TV and we decided to take a country drive, since it was raining and not suitable weather for a walk.

We drove around the far end of Lake Orange, and through the little town of Cedar Grove. It was peaceful and relaxing, with rain pattering softly on the windshield. The sky was a smudged streak of gray, yet one could see spring peeping round the corner in the bright green fields dotted with daffodils and the frilly white blossoms of pear trees.

When we returned home we had tea with Ted and watched the end of the game together (Duke won, Ted was happy!) Then Martine and I went upstairs to my study, where we chatted about the book, *Meeting Jesus Again For The First Time*, which I had recently loaned her. We talked about religion and memory, death, dying, and loneliness. Martine offered to spend the night with me if I should ever want it. It was a generous and kind offer, for she well knows that night is the hardest time for me. Apparently, one is never too old to be afraid of the dark.

March 11, 1998

I'm home alone. Ted is in the hospital, where he's been since Monday. The cancer has sent his blood sugar soaring, his skin has a slightly yellow cast, and he is having brief moments where, as he describes it, his brain meanders to another dimension. It's as though he can't always keep track of its whereabouts.

His body looks like a battleground and cancer is winning this fight; he is thin and gaunt. Yet despite the anxiety that surely accompanies these physical changes, he is resolute and cheerful, determined to meet this challenge with his usual dignity and grace.

This afternoon Ted spent the better part of an hour reading Robert Frost's poetry to me. It was like always, Ted reading aloud, while I listened contentedly as he rolled his tongue around sentences and images he loves. Yet, nothing is as it once was, nothing at all.

It's night now, dark and cold outside, and a hard frost is predicted overnight. It's a comfort to be here, in this quirky Japanese-style house that Ted built. It's familiar and reassuring, surrounding me with Ted's sensibilities and the comforting abundance of books. I wrap myself in our sheltering home, wearing it like a magical protective cloak.

March 12, 1998

I used to be profligate with time. I spent unaccountable hours lost in mindless chores or off on solitary adventures while Ted worked and read in his study. Then we would meet, late in the evening, to chat about nothing much, or Ted might relate how his class was going, or his writing, or whatever he was most enthused about that particular night.

I didn't fully recognize the value of those dear parcels of time. I didn't notice their sweetness, they seemed only the ordinary way of husbands and wives, nothing special. How was I to know it would all come to this? How could I ever have guessed that now I'd be trying to memorize Ted's face and keep the sound of his voice forever in my ear.

March 14, 1998

Ted and I were walking around the oncology unit on the ninth floor of the hospital when we passed a trash can. Ted walked over to it, and started to remove a dirty white cloth hanging from its rim. I asked what he was doing; why not leave the trash alone? He responded by saying that he had hoped the white cloth had been cleaner. He had noticed a chicken bone on the floor near where we had just passed, and he wanted to go back and deposit it in the trash. He would have done so, were the white cloth not so dirty that he feared touching it.

I could tell he was thinking about something when he turned to me and, still walking, he quietly recounted that he had read, years ago, if a person did just one thing each day to contribute to the general betterment of life, one could consider his life, at its end, to have been well-lived. He was trying to do his daily good deed by retrieving the chicken bone and putting it properly in the trash.

Advanced metastatic cancer is not enough of an excuse for him to shirk this responsibility or to forgo an opportunity to live by his inherent decency. Sometimes, I'm simply in awe of him.

March 14, 1998

Dear Charles and Susan,

I just got home from the hospital and found your card in the mailbox. Thank you for your good thoughts, your sweet concern, and especially your love.

Ted is doing OK. He was hoping to come home today but the chills and night sweats remain formidable. Dr. M has changed his medication which will hopefully make him more comfortable. It's possible he may come home tomorrow, I sure hope so. We did go out for a walk this afternoon, only around the perimeter of the hospital, but it was sunny and clear and Ted was delighted to feel the spring breeze on his cheek and to notice that the cherry trees had survived our most recent frost. He had that broad, boyish grin on his face as he examined each crabapple and cherry tree we passed. It was wonderful for him to get out, but I noticed that it tired him out considerably, that he is weaker now than he was before this hospitalization. He noticed it, too.

Yesterday's ultrasound exam showed some enlargement and irritation of the bile duct but no infection or abscess. This was as Dr. M expected. Ted is jaundiced now, his skin has a pronounced yellow cast. It is obvious the disease is advancing.

Despite all, Ted remains hopeful and utterly at ease in this precarious situation. It is quite impressive. He is, as always, unfailingly courteous to everyone. Unlike me, he never gets snappy or brusque or moody, nor has he ever once descended into anything resembling self-pity since this ordeal began. I am awed by him, privileged to witness a degree of grace and courage I can only describe as remarkable.

It will be good to see you next week. Ted is so looking forward to it. He loves you so much. I can always tell when he is talking on the phone to you because his voice changes, the words change shape and his voice takes on a velvet quality, as if he were wrapping each word in love. It will do Ted great good to see you. And me, too. We love you dearly.

Judy

March 18, 1998

Dear Professor Kato,

My apologies for not getting back to you sooner. When your letter first arrived I was scheduled to have some major medical tests in another ten days or so. I decided to wait to see the results of those tests, and whether or not my doctor thought I would be healthy enough to come to Japan in September before answering your letter. Unfortunately, the results were not encouraging. In fact, they put me in the hospital for another week, so the answer is even later than I expected it to be.

I'm out of the hospital now and some of the immediate problems are under control, but it is also clear that my condition is becoming worse and that I won't be able to accept your very kind and generous invitation.

Again, I'm sorry for the delay in getting back to you. And I'm even more sorry that I have to decline an invitation that I very much wish I could have accepted. I would have thoroughly enjoyed the opportunity to see you and Japan again. Sometimes, though, things just don't work out the way you hope they will.

On a different note, I hope all is well with you and Yukako and that you are both having a rewarding year. And when the cherry blossoms arrive, please admire them for me, too.

With best wishes,

Ted

March 21, 1998

There are smaller worlds hidden within this large world, the same way those lacquered Russian dolls each nest securely inside a larger version of itself. These worlds within worlds are hardly noticeable until, suddenly, you find yourself living in one. I recently lived in a world bounded by love and abundance. It was a splendid place which I had come to take for granted, believing, that having finally found my way there, I would stay forever, safe and happy, but I have since learned otherwise. Now I live in a gray world of sadness, a place I've been before and remember well. It is overrun with thick, listless melancholy, awash in a salty shoal of tears. I am immersed in this world the way a fish is immersed in water; it is my entire world.

I wander its border with a sorrowful heart, trying to make sense of life, but the questions I ask have no answers, there is only what is. This is a place of desolation, yet there is something else, even here. I'm not sure what to call it, but I know it is Ted's best gift to me. It keeps me from being entombed in darkness, from spinning out of control into madness and the empty void beyond. It keeps my heart from turning to stone. It will be my salvation. I think it must be love.

March 23, 1998

Through the window in my study, I watch a great blue heron stand imposingly at the lake's edge, quiet and still, while presiding over a flock of frisky ducks swimming by, as if solely for his pleasure. He appraises them with dignity as they pass downstream, much like a four-star general reviewing his troops.

Now the ducks have gone and the heron stands alone near the shore, slowly lifting one long, slender leg, then the other, doing an exquisite adagio down the shoreline as he looks for food at the water's edge. He is beautiful, otherworldly, more graceful than any ballerina. As I continue watching, the heron unfolds his majestic wings and rises slowly into the air with unspeakable lightness, riding air currents effortlessly, skimming the water with wings outstretched, until I can no longer keep him in my sight. And when he is gone, I am left to contemplate the existence of angels, for surely I have just witnessed one of God's most noble messengers.

March 31, 1998

I am surrounded now by the irrefutable evidence of resurrection. It is visible on every tree and it blooms in every flower. This is the holy time, renewal at its most fragrant. Jubilation is in the very air I breathe, as I witness the sacred cycle of life and death and life, yet again. This exuberant appearance of new life everywhere transfixes me, as the earth shakes off winter's malaise and wakes to the warmth of the sun, marveling in itself.

Songbirds have returned from their southern migrations, and baby-fresh leaves have burst from their buds. Redbud trees line the road to our house garbed in audacious fuchsia, and clusters of violets and grape hyacinths haphazardly dot the ground, leaving calling cards in purple and blue. The weeping cherry tree in our front yard is all dressed up in fluffy, girlish pink, and across the driveway two redheaded poppies dance among the daffodils, uninvited but welcome visitors. This is a feast for the senses. It is spring, hallelujah!

Spring is nature's response to winter. It makes death comprehensible, for without death there would be none of this. As spring cannot come without winter, so life cannot flourish without death. It is Sister Death, hooded and dark, who quietly nurtures the requisite elements, keeping them safe, fostering them diligently, until some miracle occurs and, once again, life begins anew.

April 1, 1998

I had bad dreams last night, dreams about waiting for Ted to die. I awoke before dawn drenched in sweat and sorrow, as I lay in bed gazing at the outline of Ted's bony body, listening to his uneven breathing. I am overwhelmed by sorrow for what might have been, for the life we could have had together, it was a life I had spent a lifetime waiting for.

Dawn is slowly brightening the sky. Outside my bedroom window, the rippling lake is ringed with trees which sway rhythmically in an early morning breeze, rustling tiny newborn leaves, while squirrels celebrate the day with acrobatics in the high limbs of oaks, and songbirds greet morning with melody. It is a hopeful scene, completely at odds with my heavy heart.

This disease is claiming Ted for death and, little by little, it is destroying his body. He is painfully thin now, without muscle or mass. Biliary obstruction has turned his skin a dismal shade of mustard, and his bright blue eyes are suspended in whites that have turned a putrid, milky yellow. His eyes look out at the world from bony sockets, his skin is stretched taut, all the bones of his face are visible. He is retaining fluids, his feet and ankles are swollen, the skin pulling tight. Elephant legs.

But he can still walk the mile to our mailbox, and he is as thoughtful and kind as ever. His mind is sharp and clear and he is not in any pain. He will reclaim his Margaret Atwood class today. He wants to finish the semester and it will be good for him to be back in the classroom. He longs to do this, but I wonder if his ghoulish appearance will be too startling, and I hope his students don't flee from the classroom, screaming with fright. That would be the worst thing for him to endure.

Notes from the Catastrophic Realm

Walking home together from our mailbox

April 4, 1998

Spring has given me its abundance like a gift. The redbud trees, in full flower, line our road like merrymakers massed at a parade. They are interspersed with dogwoods, whose demure blossoms float on leafless branches, and honeysuckle is insinuating itself everywhere. It is a glory here.

The lake is ringed with trees decked in green again, their leaves still tiny and new to the world. It is a sacrament, I am sure, to watch these baby-fresh leaves change over time, from spring's chartreuse to the rich forest color they'll assume by summer. Then, these once young leaves will turn scarlet and gold in September, lighting up the lake in a flashy display of shimmering brilliance, before tumbling and gliding and dancing down the wind to their deaths. Winter, of course, will wither everything, turning dead leaves moldy and brown, and it will become hard to recall the possibility of spring, buried beneath frozen decay.

But it is here now, just for these few brief weeks, life at its blessed best, new and hopeful, born despite winter's indifference. It is a stunning thing, emblematic of the cyclic nature of existence, a sign of God's benevolent love.

April 6, 1998

I have taken a leave of absence from work. I want to spend my time with Ted, making the most of whatever time we have together. It's what I need to do and I don't miss work in the least.

There is a large world here at the lake, where geese and ducks and herons live. It is life at its richest and I'm here to watch it all, as spring shakes the earth awake again. It's a significant thing, the changing of seasons, worthy of our notice. It cautions me to keep an eye on life and not let it slip away while my back is turned. Spring will last only a few weeks, summer will evaporate, and autumn will whirl away in a mad display of color. Then winter will, once again, lay it's icy hand over the ground. Life is but a momentary gift, easily squandered. I'm glad to be right here, holding it close, learning to discern the various textures of life and death.

Ted has been feeling well. He's teaching again, finishing his Margaret Atwood class. When he returned to the classroom last Wednesday, his students stood up, happily, tearfully, applauding his return, each one, in turn, handing him a spring flower gathered from around the campus. It was the sweetest of homecomings for him.

When the semester ends, we hope to take a trip to western Canada, specifically to Calgary, Vancouver, and of course, Mountain View. I hope we will make it, I don't assume it will happen just because we plan it. I don't ever assume tomorrow any more, but I am beginning to learn to live within uncertainty and to understand that doing so has a value all its own. It fosters gratitude and is an antidote to boredom and other end of the century ills. Quite honestly, I'm beginning to enjoy it.

April 10, 1998

I am shocked by how much I enjoy not working. I don't miss it at all, nor do I feel isolated or deprived. On the contrary, I feel I've reclaimed my own life. Even in this time of uncertainty, when death and despair skulk like hooligans in the shadows, I find deep satisfaction in fully considering life and savoring its bewildering design.

I feel like I'm seeing spring for the very first time and, maybe, I am. Day by day, I note the seasonal changes I would ordinarily not be at home to witness, or I would be too tired to notice, at the end of a long, demanding work day.

This morning I see there are new leaves on the two beech trees outside our kitchen window. They must have been coaxed from their buds by yesterday's soaking rain. Beech trees get their leaves late in the season, but now even they are wearing their seasonal best.

The dogwoods are in full bloom, sprays of unpretentious white and pink blossoms punctuate the green woods with airy beauty, and soon the irises will open. Azaleas are already adding brilliant pinks and reds to the April festivities, and I have time to watch it all, filling my heart and my senses with the sheer audacity of life resurrecting itself, right outside my door.

It might be a sin to sit in an office on a day like this, closed off from one of the greatest visual shows nature presents. It deserves our recognition, and if we scrutinize it closely, I suspect it has secrets to share and lessons to teach.

April 12, 1998

Maybe this is our miracle: Ted seems to be getting better. He is still thin and jaundiced but he is alert, active and vigorously alive. It is as though spring has breathed new life into him, as she has into every other living thing here by the lake. His increased energy is readily apparent as he cooks a Japanese curry, chopping vegetables with a gusto I thought never to see again. He eats with a rapacious appetite, and then spends long hours in his study, reading texts for class, preparing lessons, delighting in work he deems a holy trust. He returns home from teaching visibly energized and happy, while I soak up his happiness like a hedonist, shamelessly luxuriating in it. Perhaps miracles are made of stuff like this: small wonders, not too showy.

We hope to visit western Canada when the semester ends. We had planned to make this trip over the summer, but that was before our lives were reorganized by cancer, when we thought we had all the time in the world, to enjoy the world. Now, of course everything is different and we're far more conscious of the value of time, indeed, it has become our most precious treasure. Each day that Ted feels well is a welcome but astonishing surprise, so I am giddy with joy, delirious with happiness, amazed beyond words, that a small but bona fide miracle seems to be happening, right before our eyes.

April 20, 1998

Ted is less jaundiced than he was two weeks ago. Dr. M says his bilirubin level has dropped considerably and he's eating now with an insatiable appetite that's been long absent. I am thankful to whatever gods are sending us these blissful, unmarred days. I relish every hour and carefully carve the shape of each day into my mind, storing it safely away for the famine time that I know will one day come. But today, I am brimming with joy, over-flowing with gratitude for Ted's new-found vigor.

Last night, as Ted was preparing for today's class he called me into his study to share some of his favorite poems. I settled into the big gray, upholstered chair in the corner of the room, while Ted, leaning back in his chair, slipper-shod feet propped on the rim of his desk, began reading Margaret Atwood's pungent thoughts on love.

As he read, I studied his face in profile, the curved contour of his head, his brown curly hair, graying at the temples. His face retains an open, youthful quality and an air of hopefulness suggesting inner joy. This is especially evident when he reads words he loves, or hikes through the woods, finding wild fruits and berries along the way. His *joie de vivre* serves him well, enabling him to recognize true prosperity and greet the world with open-hearted delight. I think this is what faith is made of: an absolute confidence in the rightness of the universe and a joyous response to the entirety of life, not just the goodies it delivers.

April 21, 1998

My cat Asia is distracting me by sitting at my feet and staring at me hard with her golden, unblinking eyes. I know exactly what she wants: she wants me to scrunch a small piece of paper into a tiny ball and throw it, so she can retrieve it. She will play this game for hours if someone is willing to indulge her. I look down at the floor and see that she's brought over a shred of scrap paper from the waste basket to encourage me. I'm not cooperating, though.

Sometimes, I worry that I don't fully appreciate Asia. I make fun of her and often think she's stupid, but maybe it's not quite so simple. She's only stupid about things I think are important. She's quite clever about her own particular interests. She can open dresser drawers and amuse herself for hours with her own solitary games. She is independent and intrepid, and unlike her owner, she is undaunted by insects of any kind. And, of course, she is beautiful, without arrogance or self-consciousness.

I wonder what it's like to have a cat's consciousness, to view the world through eyes not human. I wonder how we seem to them, probably none too brilliant. Last night Ted and I watched a TV documentary about Siberian tigers, which are near extinct in the world. We have usurped their habitat and destroyed their environment. If the world loses the tiger, what does it signify? Is it a judgment upon us or a warning? Can we keep killing off Creation without eventually killing ourselves off, too? I hear the Canadians have begun killing baby harp seals again. I worry for the world and for the soul of humankind.

April 22, 1998

I am now officially unemployed. UNC Hospital wouldn't extend my leave of absence, not even for the five weeks of vacation I had accrued. They will, of course, pay me for that time, but as my boss, Kaye, told me, they aren't obligated to hold my position. Consequently, the health insurance I'm entitled to through COBRA will commence five weeks earlier and that eighteen month clock will end that much sooner. I'm disappointed they would make no concession to my situation. Certainly, I didn't expect them to hold my position indefinitely, but I did think they could have kept it open for five more weeks, particularly since Kaye had told me emphatically that the department wanted to do everything possible to accommodate me.

But there is also this: Mareid, our superb office manager, called specifically to suggest I use my accrued sick time this week instead of continuing my unpaid leave of absence, a suggestion that prevents me from forfeiting an entire week's salary. Later in the day, my colleagues Denise and Sally phoned, just to make sure I was OK. Though I'm leaving the job, I'm taking Mareid, Denise and Sally's friendship with me, and that's compensation enough.

Losing this job may be a blessing in disguise, forcing me to consider a different direction when it's time to go back to work. Although I've enjoyed being a risk manager, it has always made me slightly uneasy. In my heart, I knew I didn't belong there any more than I belonged in a medical defense law firm, a job I also enjoyed for the six years I did it in New York City. But I no longer belong in an open heart operating room either, not in these days of managed care, when operating room nursing is more like working on a factory assembly line than anything else. Perhaps I simply don't want to devote forty hours a week (and more) to any job. I love enjoying the stillness of mornings at the lake, carefully observing the arc of each day, and I treasure the autonomy of making my own decisions about how to spend my time, the exquisite privilege of being the author of my own day.

April 25, 1998

Ted had his final chemotherapy treatment last Thursday. His bilirubin level continues to decrease and he is correspondingly less jaundiced. He feels well and is brimming with vitality and optimism. I am hopeful these improvements will be reflected in the results of his upcoming MRI, and that we can anticipate further improvement with continued chemotherapy cycles.

Because of this great good luck, we have the opportunity to engage in ordinary life once again. We've been visiting friends, dining out, exploring the lake from our canoe, and monitoring the growth of Ted's beloved berry bushes and fruit trees behind the house. We have the beginnings of black raspberries, currants, gooseberries, grapes, blueberries and, of course, wild strawberries.

Our next door neighbor will likely have a large crop of tart cherries and we are hoping for an abundance of persimmons, pears, and peaches. Ted has discovered a wild plum tree growing along Lake Orange Road which has flowered lavishly, and he's eager to see if it bears fruit. He talks about replenishing our vanishing stock of jams and jellies this summer.

Ted's jam is tastier than store-bought varieties, superior even to the fancy imported brands lining the shelves of Chapel Hill's best markets, but it has significance for other reasons, too. It's indicative of his appreciation for the gifts of the everyday, a tangible connection to his past, linking him to his mother and grandmother, the women who taught him to can as a boy on an isolated Alberta ranch.

I want the jam available to me and Charles, labeled in Ted's own hand, for the time when he will no longer be with us. We will need it desperately then, along with the umishu liqueur Ted makes from wild grapes. They will serve as a communion of sorts, a way for us to keep him close when he's gone, a way to absorb him into ourselves, the sweet, soothing taste of love recalled.

April 28, 1998

What is most disturbing about the way my resignation has played out is Kaye's dishonesty. I realize she couldn't hold my position open forever, and certainly the consequences of my taking a family medical leave of absence should fall to me, but I can't help but feel that a small measure of compassion might have been in order. I'm particularly disappointed since she told me, when Ted was first diagnosed, that she didn't want me to worry about losing my job as well as my husband. Now those words seem empty. She did nothing for me, other than grant an unpaid leave she was mandated by law to provide. The letter she sent me to memorialize our last conversation, during which she informed me I either had to return to work or resign by April 28th was disingenuous and self-serving. It suggested that favors had been granted and accommodations had been made, that a degree of compassion had been shown for my unenviable situation. In fact, none had, and the letter cast her in a better light than she deserved. It was a letter calculated to make Kaye seem as though she had done everything possible to help an employee, but the reality, known to both of us, is that she did no such thing.

I'm concerned about the work culture in this country. Kaye is by anyone's definition a workaholic, rigidly bound to the rules and values of management. She suffers from an inability to modulate her life with anything resembling common sense and her identity is completely bound up in her management position. Our philosophies of work have been at odds since I began working there. Kaye's career is the biggest part of her life and she wants her employees to hold similar values, but I prefer building a life to having a career become the focal point of my existence. A career has always been secondary to me, something I tailor to fit the larger whole, which to my mind, is no less than formulating a thoughtful response to the question of what it means to be alive and human on this earth. Still, we always got along well, Kaye and I, respecting each other's ability to do an often difficult job.

April 29, 1998

I had chores to do this morning, but after I finished, and before Martine came by to visit, I went to the barn to see Lucky. After a hard winter, he is finally gaining weight and shedding out. An equine dentist treated him several weeks ago, and since then he's been dropping less grain and seems to be in better spirits. Dental problems prevented him from maintaining his weight this winter, and by February he had lost so much weight that he looked unfit and old beyond his years. The regular vet floated his teeth more than once, but failed to remedy, or even diagnose the problem. Lucky's shaggy winter coat turned coarse and dull, and it became obvious he wasn't well, which was very disturbing. Now, thanks to the ministrations of this equine dentist, who corrected a problem that still remains mysterious, Lucky is gaining weight and muscle tone, and his new spring coat is coming in all silver and soft. He is alert and playful once again, showing off buoyant gaits and exuberant bursts of equine energy.

I watch as Lucky careens around the perimeter of the large paddock at a full-out gallop, just for the fun of it, his long white tail streaming behind him like a flag, his hooves pounding a syncopated rhythm into the air. Every toned and rippling muscle in his body flexes and releases, contracts and expands, propelling him along the fence line with the power and speed of a rocket and the elegance of an athlete.

I'm always just the tiniest bit surprised when he finally stops still, then prances and jigs over to the fence where I stand, my feet planted on the lowest rail, my body leaning over, reaching out with both arms to embrace his muscular neck and smell his fresh, frothy fragrance. It's a startling realization, this recognition that I share a bond with this beautiful and majestic creature, that something akin to friendship or even love, binds us together in a deeply meaningful way.

May 5, 1998

All winter long, the weeping cherry tree stood at the entrance to our driveway, spindly and barren, limbs drooping almost to the ground. I saw it every morning when I left for work, and then again, upon my return home at the end of the day. It looked as forlorn as I felt, blending into the bleak, brown landscape.

In early April, however, our weeping cherry welcomed spring with stunning fervor, its bowed branches newly attired in fluffy pink blossoms that danced with every passing breeze, and when lit from behind by the sun, it shimmered with a golden halo of dispersed sunbeams. Our artist friend, Gerrit, came to visit from California just when it achieved its fullest bloom, and he recognized immediately that this was something special.

Come April's end, the cherry tree shed its glitzy beauty as its tiny pink petals fluttered to the ground with the daintiness of falling snowflakes and, one by one, were replaced with leaves of a decidedly matronly shade of green. Gerrit reluctantly left us, returning home to his studio by the sea, carrying memories and photos of a voluptuous North Carolina spring.

While gazing out at the placid Pacific, facing a blank canvas, Gerrit evidently recalled the glory days of our weeping cherry tree, and after turning the memory over in his mind a time or two, he transformed it into art. When he finished, he packed the work in a large wooden crate and sent it to me and Ted.

When we unpacked the crate and turned the large canvas around, we were astonished by what we saw: color and form swirled into fiery, textured shapes of orange, green, yellow, and pink, all alluding to the enduring mystery of renewal, and pulsating with such intense energy that it seemed as alive as the living tree. Now the painting hangs over the mantle in our living room, illuminating everything.

Our Weeping Cherry Tree

The weeping cherry tree, by Gerrit Greve

THE RETURN

When I come back I think I'll be
A ghost you feel but cannot see.
A groping ghost, whose fingers ply
The curve of breast, the top of thigh.

But all will not to teasing tend,
I'll rub your back for hours on end.
And even in your dreams you'll know
I hold you tight and won't let go.

Ted Davidson
6.98

June 22, 1998

It's summer, officially, and it's appropriately hot and humid here. Leaves fan themselves on infrequent breezes and mosquitoes buzz happily about, far more active than most other life forms. It has been a special time for me and Ted.

We have been given a reprieve, a gift of days, a space in which to enjoy life and put aside the serious business of cancer. I have no idea how long this interlude will last. I hope it continues forever, but I know it could well end tomorrow. We are both painfully aware of the tenuous nature of life, how easily one can slip out of it, into illness, death and beyond. Now, life seems an exquisite thing, as fragile as a wren's egg.

Saturday is Ted's sixty-second birthday. Last March, I wouldn't have thought he'd be here to celebrate it, but here we are, amazed by our good fortune. We're marking the occasion with a sumptuous dinner at *The Fearrington Inn*, celebrating with good food, good wine and all the gratitude in our hearts. We could not have been given a better gift, and however long it lasts, we are determined to enjoy every day of it.

Alas, Ted is more adept at this than I am. I try too hard to interpret the meaning inscribed in every pain, every chill, every reminder that the cancer is still hibernating in Ted's abdomen, but he doesn't worry about what will happen. He sensibly points out that worrying won't change anything, and he isn't afraid of either death or dying. Ted considers death to be the end of life as we experience it, a transition to another way of being in the universe. He doesn't view it as inherently frightening, but intuits it to be a spontaneous disconnection between body and spirit, the soul's release from the limits of incarnation, as right as rain, as natural as the summer sun.

So for now, we are simply watching summer spin a languorous spell over the lake, noticing when the waterlilies open and close each day, enjoying the spectacle of a sunset while drifting down the lake in our old canoe, happily sharing the water with a mama goose gliding silently downstream, her gaggle of fuzzy goslings following dutifully behind, paddling as fast as their little webbed feet allow.

June 23, 1998

I haven't written anything about our holiday in Alberta. I was too busy enjoying it to keep up this diary, but the trip was a success, a homecoming for Ted and an opportunity for me to be embraced by this wonderful family I see too infrequently. In addition, we got to meet Renee, the woman who bred both Digger and Desi, the Davidson bullmastiffs.

Karen and her husband Roy met us at the Calgary airport and bundled us back to their home, where Charles and Susan (who had arrived the day before), Karen's daughter, Jo, and her husband, Frank, all awaited our arrival. Digger, of course, was there too, offering his own robust and slobbering greeting.

Karen had rented a small van to transport us all on an excursion to the mountain lakes of the Kananaskis region. Our first stop, however, was to the town of Drumheller to meet Renee, bullmastiff breeder extaordinaire, who had an eight-month-old puppy Ted and I could have for a reasonable price. I was pretty sure I wanted a younger puppy and doubted an eight-month-old would appeal to me, despite Karen's assertion that this pup had the prettiest face and coat of any bullmastiff she'd ever seen. Renee originally planned to keep her for the show ring but as she grew, her top line developed slightly less than straight, hence, Renee's decision to find her a pet home. It wouldn't hurt to meet this dog, I considered, and we might also ask if Renee could send us a younger puppy from the next available litter.

Renee was a large woman with an open manner and a face that so resembled Ludwig von Beethoven she might have been his long-lost Canadian descendent. Shortly after our arrival, after greetings and introductions were made all around, we walked together to the kennel area, where Renee introduced us to Sophie, a sweet-faced, eighty-five pound, eight-month-old, red bullmastiff pup. She had a small driblet of white fur that spilled down her neck fanning out to form a white puddle on her chest, and her tail wagged constantly. Renee threw a leash and collar over her head, led her out of the kennel, and handed the leash to me. Off we went, just me and Sophie, ambling down Renee's long gravel driveway. Sophie bounced along next to me, exuding a degree of puppy joy that could hardly be contained. Her chestnut coat glowed in the summer sun and her playful curiosity was infectious and endearing. While everyone else retreated to Renee's porch for iced tea and biscuits, Sophie and I frolicked, liked two children, on Renee's spacious, grassy front yard. She hopped, skipped and pranced playfully by my side, deciphering the air with her nose, greeting clusters of shrubs with play-bows, occasionally stopping dead to turn and look up at me, her winsome brown eyes expressing intelligence and trust. It would have taken someone with a heart harder than mine to resist falling in love with this charming creature. When we finally sauntered back to the group, now fast friends, Ted looked at me, broke out in a grin, and said,

"I can see we have a dog to get back home."

We arranged to retrieve Sophie from Renee's kennel the day before our flight home, and after I reluctantly said a temporary good-by to my new best friend, we piled back into the van, and left for Horseshoe Canyon in the Alberta Badlands, where the prairie drops off precipitously, and one finds oneself looking straight down into a sprawling vista of prehistoric terrain. Dinosaurs once roamed this landscape and, indeed, dinosaur fossils are still found here in abundance. After a thorough exploration, we went to the dinosaur museum, where we eyed various prehistoric relics and viewed intriguing exhibits of imagined dinosaur family life.

Next, it was on to the Kananaskis region. Karen noted there was less snow in the mountains than usual, confirmation that spring had come early and mild. We parked the van high in the mountains, deciding to walk beside a small crystalline mountain lake still partially frozen and reflecting sunlight, like a mirror, onto the encircling mountains. Ted found Karen a "Brancusi," a shapely piece of driftwood sculpture washed up from the lake, and we all (including Digger) clowned, posed, and mugged for the cameras.

From there, we drove to *Waterton Lakes National Park,* where Ted's dad used to summer pasture his cattle, back when ranchers were permitted to do so. Ted had spent many summer days and nights at *Waterton.* It was the place to go to on a Saturday night, the best place to meet girls, to be young, to have fun. He spent an entire summer there one year with his aunt and uncle, who owned a cabin in the park, and ran the local gas station. Both the cabin and the gas station remain, but Ted's aunt and uncle are long gone. We were lucky enough to spend three nights in a charming park cabin, owned by Jo's in laws.

Late one morning, Jo, Ted and I took the short walk from the cabin to the nearby local candy store, picking up sugary treats for all. It was the same store Ted had frequented decades ago, and little about it had changed. Later, we piled into the van, bags of candy in hand, to visit the buffalo paddock, where we gawked at buffalo cows with their bulky babies, and further on we saw mountain sheep, mountain goats, and large herds of elk lazily grazing on young spring grass. Each day, we rose to the warmth of bright sunshine and inhaled the sweet fragrance of fresh mountain air.

After returning to Calgary, we spent a day downtown with Karen, exploring local Native art galleries. Ted bought me a small soapstone sculpture of a bird with a particularly pleasing eye, and we bought my brother Joel a huge dream-catcher (for his out-sized dreams) and a more restrained version for Martine.

After a week at Karen and Roy's, we flew to Vancouver, along with Karen, Charles and Susan. We all stayed at Kennie's house, pretty much taking it over. Kennie gave us a grand tour of the city, and cooked up some tasty Pacific salmon for us, as well. Vancouver is one of the beautiful cities of the world, a civilized gem, where greenery and flowers abound and color saturates everything. It's an energetic city that cultivates Canadian civility, while throbbing with the cosmopolitan sophistication one expects in a city poised on the edge of the Pacific ocean.

We had several visits with Ted's dad, who lives in a small apartment in a fashionable section of the city. On one occasion, he whisked us all off to a fabulous lunch at his favorite restaurant, the inimitable *William Tell*. Everyone there knew Olaf and treated him like the courtly gentleman he is. In his honor, they prepared a special, delicious feast for all of us.

But it was when our visit was drawing to a close, when it was time for Olaf to bid Ted good-by that he exposed his true feelings and gave free reign to his love. With tears coursing down his weathered, wrinkled face, Olaf clutched Ted in a tight embrace, saying he knew this would be their last good-by. Then he looked Ted directly in the eye and said that he had always been proud of him, but never more than now. It was deeply moving.

Upon returning to Calgary, Karen and Roy drove us back to Renee's house where we picked up Sophie, along with her traveling papers and crate. Early the next morning we boarded a plane and headed home.

Although our trip home was long, it was happily uneventful, and Sophie proved to be a real trooper, making it on to all three planes without mishap. After twelve hours, when she disembarked at the Raleigh-Durham airport, she was none the worse for her adventure, her tail wagging wildly as we clipped a leash to her collar and she trotted out of the crate and into the airport terminal.

It was a happy homecoming, indeed, at 4416 Arrowhead Trail. It was good to see the kitties again, though they were somewhat startled to meet Sophie, who learned almost instantaneously (after Asia hissed maniacally at her) never to chase a kitty. It was a great trip, but it's also good to be home. Several months ago, when Ted was so ill, I wouldn't have imagined any of this possible, and I am grateful beyond telling, for every day of it.

A Love Story

Sophie

Spoken Meditation, June 28, 1998
Community Church of Chapel Hill, UU

There are miracles here waiting for us to notice them. They send discreet invitations suggesting we peek into places where our biography is written in cryptogram by leafy trees that sway to the rhythms of life and death, but we are too distracted as we drive to work on asphalt highways, or shuffle children between school and soccer, or shop at malls for consumer goods to fill the emptiness at our core.

Now the trees wear modest June leaves and a stately calm, murmuring polite messages to passing summer breezes about the passage of time, but soon they will shake their branches and shout impatiently. Dressed in autumn's Technicolor attire, they will implore insistently that we seek a sharper awareness, realize our time here is finite, recognize the miracle it is that any one of us is here, right now, alive, on this spinning planet. The universe does its best to remind us that life is a gift, not a promise, but as we hack through a jungle of mind-numbing routine, we fail to observe that we are, indeed, surrounded by miracles and immersed in wonders.

So give yourself an hour, or a morning, or an evening, when the summer sun floats down the western sky. Look around and see, as if for the first time, that the lilies are in bloom. Applaud the squirrels as they perform stunning feats of aerial acrobatics in your backyard, high in the canopy of the treetops. Relax in a warm bath, in a room lit by a flickering aromatic candle, and listen to the calm of your own breathing. Keep time to the rhythm of your pulse and consider that we are part of a throbbing, vibrant universe, cradled by earth, made of stardust, linked to the pull of the moon and the ebb and flow of tides. Reclaim your ability to notice life's abundance and bear witness to the continuing miracle of Creation.

July 7, 1998

It's been hectic here, so I'm stealing a few minutes of peace and quiet. Ted's friends, George and Pam, are visiting from Michigan, and when they leave, we'll be going to Georgia to visit my brothers, Joel and Aaron. Ted's students and friends have been coming to the house with regularity, and although it's wonderful to see these dear friends, it is also tiring. More than Ted, I need to replenish myself with solitude. I crave time alone with Sophie, Lucky, Asia and Tilla to reinvigorate my soul.

This morning Sophie and I walked to the red horse barn where we saw a great blue heron sunning itself lazily on the pond's dock. Disturbed by our intrusion, he unfolded his imposing wings and silently arose from the dock with a feathery shiver, gliding across the silvered pond, then flying into the hidden heights of nearby treetops. It was magical, like a glimpse of the Eternal, and both Sophie and I watched with awe and fascination.

These summer days have been mercilessly hot, and the long sultry afternoons are often punctuated by brief thunderstorms that barely make a dent in the thick, heavy air. Yet time is racing by, galloping hard, like a runaway horse. Summer will be over in a flash, and I'm not particularly looking forward to the future. I'm trying to balance myself on a thin high-wire, raised midway between illness and health, fear and gratitude. I'm scared of the future, preferring to remain right here, forever, but there is nothing I can do to prevent tomorrow's arrival. I can only enjoy the days we have been given and trust that the future will open itself gently to us.

For Judy
    On Time

I hope I have a chance to see
What time can do to you, to me:
One wrinkled woman, one bent man
Who face no future, hand in hand.

But if we have then, just our past,
It still will show how love can last.
And brief or long as life may be
Our love is for Eternity.

Ted Davidson, 7/98

July 13, 1998

Two days before my 51ˢᵗ birthday

It's hard for me to look back across decades and view the expanse of my own life. There are holes and blank spots where memory should be, so I hardly understand how I became the woman I am now. I can't quite grasp hold of the girl I used to be, because I shed that life as dispassionately as a snake sheds its skin, without remorse, keeping only a memento of sadness right behind my eyes to remind me that I used to be an unhappy child.

    I was the girl with straight brown hair, cropped short so it wouldn't be bothersome for my mother. Freckles marched across my nose in summer, and I was tall, with skinny arms and too long legs. I dressed in unstylish clothing, out of touch with fashion trends. My mother was oblivious to such things, considering them unimportant, so I wore shoes good for growing feet, but all wrong for a young girl wanting to fit in with popular girls who bought their clothes in department stores. Mine were made by a dressmaker and though they were well tailored, they were, to my mind, dowdy.

    My life was circumscribed by school, synagogue, and the several blocks of middle class neighborhood in which we lived. It was a cohesive neighborhood and, from the beginning, I had good friends there, but I remained on the perimeter of social groups, never quite a wholehearted participant, though never excluded, either. My mother and I were often at odds and always on tenterhooks, waiting for the next disagreement, plotting our battle moves as we circled around one another with unnatural wariness.

    I wonder now, with childhood safely in my past, what I would be like if my young years had been different, if I had had a loving mother teaching me everything a young girl should know. Who would I be now if I had received that wholeness a mother lovingly bestows on her child? Such a profound sense of well-being can't be duplicated or obtained later in life, it can only be compensated for, and though I am the grateful recipient of much loving compensation, I missed out on that most primal relationship, and so, alas, did my mother.

August 5, 1998

We have been given a reprieve from illness, and the specter of death has receded into the background of our lives. Instead of the poverty of sickness, we find ourselves, once again, immersed in the abundance of life and vigor.

We are using this time well, being careful not to squander it in hand-wringing over the future. Instead, we take each day, one by one, and turn it over in our hands, examining its unique qualities as though it were a jewel, worthy of care. Over the past few months, we have grown more conscious of each day's worth and of the sustenance we draw from it and from each other, but we have also learned to take nothing for granted, and to keep both eyes open. Even our daily chores have taken on a specialness, and anything we do together has earned new value and meaning.

We know our good fortune will not last forever. Ted may suddenly and quickly succumb to this cancer, and though that thought causes me considerable anxiety, it's neither sensible nor productive to dwell on it. I don't want to lose to either fear or worry what I have been so unexpectedly given, so I will ride this horse, keeping a steady hold on the reins as we gallop toward our future. Life will take Ted and I where we are meant to go, and we will find the capacity to move forward.

I wonder now about the essence of life and the nature of death, if death exists at all, or if it might be a passage, not so unlike birth. Whatever comes next, all I can do is honor life as I experience it, and wait for answers to make themselves apparent in due course.

August 12, 1998

Tomorrow we are off to Ontario to visit Charles and Susan and see, with our own eyes, their beautiful new kitchen. They have completed the renovation of their old stone house, the kitchen being the most extensive and final project. Several months ago, I gave them ten thousand dollars to purchase the granite counter tops they wanted. Susan tells us they're gorgeous, and tomorrow we'll get to see them.

It will be a wonderful trip; we haven't seen Charles and Susan since May, and I can hardly wait for them to see how vigorous and healthy Ted looks. Ted is eager to go berry picking with Charles, and I'm eager to have them whip up a batch of fresh fruit jam. Susan's little niece, Emmaline, will be visiting too, and I'm hoping we get a chance to visit with Susan's Aunt Irene. I am looking forward to every bit of it.

When we return home next week, I'm going to begin looking for a part-time job since Ted will return to work in September. Yet this cancer casts a long shadow, and when Ted is at home I want to be with him, so I will only work on Monday and Wednesday, the days Ted will teach. We have no idea when this hiatus from illness will end, but we know it won't last forever, so spending time together has become our priority. Even so, it will be good for me to be out in the world again, earning a little money, and doing something society deems valuable.

August 13, 1998

It's the middle of August already, and the trees are wearing their deep summer greens. Their heavy limbs rustle like taffeta whenever a hot breeze blows across the lake. Sunlight abounds, harsh and white at mid-day, then giving way to a soft amber tint as day gives itself over to the beginning of evening. Life is everywhere here, busy in its own pursuits. There are worlds to watch by the lake, and in the woods there's a whole variety of living things to observe. The trees and the creatures who share this place with me are good teachers, offering free instruction in how to live the good life and be present in the moment.

Ted and I have enjoyed the summer. I didn't think it would be this way last March when he was tottering on the brink of liver failure. I was sure he would die before spring, missing that annual festivity, but I was wrong; instead, he got stronger each month, incorporating the vigor of the season into his own body. It feels like a small miracle.

Now autumn approaches, and soon I will be watching the squirrels prepare for winter, and the geese depart the lake in V-formation as they head to warmer climes. The slanted autumn sun will tint the whole landscape a rosy gold, and, of course, there will be the leaves, giving their own bravura performance before winter's curtain descends.

I face winter with trepidation. It has always been my least favorite season, not so much for the cold, as the dark. I hate the amputated days and miss the sun's golden comfort. Night scares me, and like a child I see goblins hidden in its long, distorted shadows, and death slithering through the darkness. I hope winter won't steal Ted's energy, and I pray we will be here together to see the cherry tree bloom next April.

August 29, 1998

Sophie, Asia and I are alone this afternoon. Ted went to his office at Duke, and Tilla is outside in the woods doing whatever it is kitties do on a hot afternoon. I have been in my study, slumped in my overstuffed recliner, reading *Alias Grace* by Margaret Atwood, with Asia curled in my lap, and Sophie asleep on the rug beside me.

Sophie is a noisy sleeper, exhaling raggedy little snores and breathing heavily. She has animated doggie dreams during which she barks and makes attenuated running movements, sometimes she even growls, which is quite amazing, since she's never growled when awake in all the time we've had her. I try to imagine what she dreams, what it is she's chasing round the bend of her canine mind, but I cannot. I wonder if her dreams are pleasant or frightening, and if she will awaken in an extravagantly good mood because she has been victorious at the chase.

Sophie is essentially foreign to me, representative of the Other, as are Tilla, Asia and Lucky, yet they are among my closest friends and I love them beyond telling. I have always had an affinity for animals, feeling a primary connection to them, even when I was very young and forbidden by my mother to keep any pets. I instinctively understood, even then, that we are here on this earth in relationship, mysteriously bound to one another into something remarkable that feels a lot like family.

September 2, 1998

It's September and summer is disappearing, evaporating in air that is thinner, less dense than it was even a few weeks ago. The leaves have begun turning from green to gold, and one already finds them twirling down a light wind to the ground. Soon there will be a tumbling blizzard of leaves dancing their final vivace, pirouetting through space, ending brief, successful leaf-lives in a riotous display of color. They fall full of confidence to their destiny, as though they trust in nature's wisdom.

Ted is back at work, just as he has been each previous September, but this year is different. This year we stand in amazement and gratitude that he is again back in the classroom. Cancer has made us more diligent and far less casual about the passage of time. Now we stand in time, marveling at our presence here, and like the leaves, we too are beginning to trust in God's compassion.

September 3, 1998

The fall term began Monday and Ted returned to work. Although he always believed he would teach this semester, I was less certain. I wasn't sure he would even be alive now, much less teaching two courses. When he talked last April about returning to school after the summer, I made the appropriate encouraging comments but, in my heart, I doubted it would happen, and yet here we are, still among the living. It makes one wonder.

Although physicians exude confidence in their expert knowledge, and medical science promotes itself without end, there is so much that is unknown. There are questions science cannot answer, and mystery floats serenely through our lives unperturbed by experts.

I don't know why Ted didn't die last March. It certainly appeared as though he would. Perhaps the chemotherapy (which neither the oncologist nor anyone else expected would do much good) found a uniquely susceptible tumor, or maybe Coyote, high in the Canadian Rockies, howled at the moon scaring the cancer away. It might have been the vial of holy water friends brought us from the river Jordan, or the Navajo healing ceremony done on Ted's behalf. Perhaps it was the perfect combination of all the above, or maybe love and will are greater healing agents than we know.

Ted's attitude toward this disease has been extraordinary. His calm acceptance and his profound belief in the goodness of the universe have girded him with emotional and spiritual strength. He is not afraid of this cancer. It cannot hurt him, even though it will probably kill him. He lives within the enduring embrace of God, or The Great Spirit, or Love, or whatever it is that orders the universe, calling down life, and shape, and color. He is more curious than afraid of death, although he is loathe to relinquish an experience as rich as his own life.

I wonder if love can keep someone alive. There is something that passes between me and Ted that I can almost feel. It crackles in the air like lightning when we sit next to each other on the sofa, while we watch television, or when we play silly games with Tilla, Asia and Sophie. It is there when we walk, hand in hand, down the road to the mailbox, or to the lake to enjoy the waterlilies. I feel it like a magnetic force binding us together, a real and physical thing. Perhaps love itself can make one whole and keep a cancer at bay. It would not be the strangest thing.

September 6, 1998

We took a walk and picked grapes this afternoon. Ted, Sophie and I scouted the shoulders of Arrowhead Trail, finding thick tangles of vines laden with large, wild, purple grapes. We picked two bags full, and then, walking further along the trail through the woods, we noticed another cluster of vines. Ted was ecstatic and we picked as many as we could reach. Then, so he could reach the very highest vines, Ted climbed onto the narrow ledge of a low cement wall separating the trail from a ravine on the other side. I preferred that Ted not risk his life straining to grab a few more grapes, but he was having such fun, and he promised to be careful, so I simply looked away and let him be. He picked half again as many grapes as before, while balancing tentatively atop the wall.

Now Ted is in the kitchen turning our grapes into jelly. He stands by the stove, like an alchemist, boiling up jam jars, squeezing grapes through an old hankie, simmering juice in large metal pots. He adds sugar and sure-jell and tastes and stirs while pots boil and steam rises, waiting for the moment when the juice will be transformed into a jewel-like jelly, amethyst in color.

He is happy doing this, and I am happy observing his happiness. It is bliss to live with this man who teaches me so much and loves me so well. He is a special one, a remarkable man who talks of Sophocles and the redemptive story of Oedipus, who can ride a horse, and parse a sentence, write a poem and make sweet jams and jellies from fruit he finds hanging in the air.

September 10, 1998

One senses autumn in this ripe afternoon air, and in the way the sun is gilding everything with a wash of muted September light. Ted is at the oncology clinic getting his weekly chemotherapy treatment while I am here, behind the house, relaxing in the grass, enjoying the sun's warmth, with Sophie and Tilla as companions. Sophie's big head is heavy on my leg, which she's using as a pillow, as she snores softly. Tilla snoozes next to her, deep in the bliss of his zillionth cat nap of the day, eyes closed tight, his agile body curled into a tight black ball.

I've noticed a perfect spider web, daintily crocheted in silk across the lowest limbs of a nearby pine, and then I spy a spindly daddy long legs, standing right next to the web, as if waiting at a bus stop. I watch with concern as he steps out, embarking on a journey that veers treacherously close to where Sophie and Tilla sleep. He scuttles across my path on rickety, hair-like legs, making his way through lush grass, traveling with determination towards the woods. I fear that either Sophie or Tilla will awaken, but this tiny solitary being skitters along, determined, and blissfully unaware of the mortal dangers that lay lurking in his path. Now he is only centimeters away from Sophie's nose, as, inch by inch, he forges ahead. I hold my breath, praying Tilla and Sophie remain asleep until he is safely past. And all the while, keeping to his task, this intrepid little insect picks his way through the grass until, finally, he disappears into the loamy woods, and I exhale with relief, glad his diligence has been rewarded. It's reassuring that, despite our blundering blindness, from time to time life blesses us with unmerited, often unrecognized good fortune, and we continue our journey unaware, never even knowing that benevolence has tenderly kissed our cheek and kept us safe from harm.

Sophie and me in the backyard

September 16, 1998

Several days ago, Ted began to have mild, intermittent back pain. It isn't particularly uncomfortable but it's definitely present and we don't know why. My fear, of course, is that the cancer has grown, or perhaps metastasized to the bone. Today is Ted's chemotherapy day and he will definitely tell the nurse practitioner about it, but because he saw Dr. M last week (for the first time in many weeks) he will not see the doctor today. I think Ted needs an MRI, and I will instruct him to request this from the nurse practitioner. He hasn't had one since last April, and we need to know what's happening, even if it's news we don't particularly want to hear.

Last night we sat in the living room, in front of Gerrit's painting of the cherry tree, eating wedges of cantaloupe, and talking candidly about the possibility that this pain could indicate disease progression. Ted is concerned, but unafraid and hoping for the best. We discussed my financial worries, especially in light of the instability of the stock market and my unemployment. I'm concerned about my ability to carry on financially without Ted, and wonder whether I could find a job that would permit me to maintain this house and keep Lucky. Ted thinks I'll be all right if I work part time, barring a national economic disaster.

Of equal concern is how I would manage in other ways in the event of Ted's death. I can't bear to think of life without him, and I get angry at the unfairness of it. Yet, as Ted points out, the same fate that gave him cancer also gave him me, so how can he shake an angry fist at fate?

"I didn't say why me when all the good stuff was happening, and I don't think that's an appropriate response to this situation either," Ted explains.

And it's true that both of us have had far more good luck than bad in our lives, and life is sometimes hard, and death will come for each of us. It is simply the way life works.

Maybe this will prove to be a false alarm, but if it isn't, I would be wise to keep in mind that success in life isn't measured by the number of one's years or the worth of one's material possessions. It is measured by how one chooses to meet each day.

September 17, 1998

Ted had his chemotherapy today, as well as a brief chat with Dr. M about the back pain he developed earlier this week. Dr. M is attributing the pain to excess stomach acid and he gave Ted a prescription for medication to alleviate it. I hope Dr. M is correct and the pain subsides, but if it doesn't, next week I'll insist on an MRI to determine its source.

I didn't get the job I applied for at the Literacy Council and I'm disappointed. It would have been work I would have enjoyed, but it pales in importance to Ted's health. If his back pain proves to be of consequence I don't want to be working, so I may postpone my job search until we have more information about the pain's etiology.

Charles arrives tonight for a quick visit. He decided to come yesterday and was able to get a cheap ticket only because the strike at Canadian Airlines suddenly ended. It's a happy surprise, and Ted is eager to see him. I'm delighted, too. It will be the first time Charles sees Sophie at home. He'll have fun with her, for sure. She's such a big, silly, loving marshmallow.

September 22, 1998

The days go on, and I'm trying not to obsess over Ted's condition. His back pain has subsided, but a residual stiffening remains. It makes me worry that the disease is progressing.
    I called Dr. M's office yesterday to request an MRI for Ted. It would give us definitive information about tumor growth, and it's been five months since his last one. We need to know if this tumor is growing so we can plan our lives accordingly, but my interactions with Dr. M's office were less than satisfactory. I spoke to the triage nurse who only focused on the fact of Ted's back pain, and insisted on phoning a prescription to our pharmacy for pain medication that Ted didn't need. I explained that Ted's pain level was negligible, and our concern was the source of the pain, not its intensity, but she wouldn't listen, insisting on forging ahead with her own agenda. She declined to let me speak to Dr. M, assuring me that she would consult with him about the MRI, and get back to me with his response. She never did. She was a gatekeeper of the worst variety. It's probably best for me to wait until Thursday when Ted has his next chemotherapy treatment, and speak to Dr. M at that time. If I call Ms. Triage Nurse now, I'll only get angry and accomplish nothing, but I want Ted to have an MRI and I will insist on it.
    It would be nice to feel that Dr. M and his colleagues were more than highly educated technicians, bulldozing their way through an arduous daily schedule. They have hardly a moment to talk to their patients, and at each encounter one feels their tension, as well as their determination to make it through a grueling day. It must be a dreadful way to practice medicine, and it is certainly demoralizing for the patient and family to be objectified by such an industrialized, assembly line process.

The good news is that Ted feels well and is happily reading his graduate student's dissertation and preparing for his own classes. He doesn't let the possibility of disease progression diminish his enjoyment of life in the here and now, instead he lives intentionally, with gusto and pleasure.

Last night at dinner we had *Bryer's Chocolate Chip Cookie Dough* ice-cream for dessert. I had bought it in error, thinking it was *Pralines and Cream*. Neither of us like it very much. The ice-cream is fine but the cookie dough chunks are yucky, and we have both been picking them out and discarding them. Last night, though, Ted gathered all his leftover cookie dough bits, formed them into a cookie and baked it in the toaster-oven. It turned into a delicious cookie, indeed, so now he will bake all his ice-cream dough bits into cookies, and is feeling quite smug and pleased with himself. Who but Ted would have thought to do this, I cannot imagine.

September 24, 1998

It's clear and pristine this morning. The sun is pale yellow and the air is spiced with an autumnal chill. It is quiet on our road, only Sophie and I, on our morning walk, disturb the peacefulness. Soon the woods will be bare of leaves, but now they are still dense and green. I inhale the ripe aroma of fall, a scent of pine and mature leaves that is carried on every fickle breeze. Summer has disappeared, and now it is only a matter of time until leaves tumble and squirrels end their play to prepare, in earnest, for the coming of winter. Already, I have seen migrations of geese, high in the sky, navigating their way southward.

It's important to me to notice the changing of the seasons and the way time moves in an arc across all life. It makes me wonder about the nature of reality and how it seems a layered thing. For now, one can only guess about ultimate reality and appreciate the gift of life in this Eden we are part of here, suspended in time between birth and death.

When I am quiet in my heart, when I look deeply into Tilla's eyes, sometimes I glimpse something that, in my mind, I know is God. And this is the heart of the Mystery, God, which is also love.

September 27, 1998

The sun is warm and inviting, modest breezes make the leaves shimmy intermittently, while a rustling murmur, like a softly played tambourine, echoes through the treetops. Down in New Orleans, however, they nervously await the arrival of hurricane George, which threatens the city with storm surges, hundred-mile-an-hour winds, and thirty inches of rain. Life is no static thing. It changes shape and keeps us guessing, and we are never quite sure which aspect of it will greet us on any given morning.

I imagine holding all of life in one hand, like a small stone, noting how smooth it is in some places, and how gritty it feels in others. Life is a hard, enduring thing, an impenetrable treasure I can never fully understand, but it has been given to me and every other living thing, like a gift, so I have something in common with the trees, and the birds, and the spiders that have, of late, been spinning artful webs in the breezeway of our house.

We are all in the same boat, living out our species-specific lives because that is what we know to do. Yet, I wonder if the leaves are frightened by their yearly fall, or if spiders pause, while wrapping their daily catch in silk, to ponder how death will come for them. They do not appear to think about such things, or perhaps they pay closer attention to life, listening more attentively to its pulse than I do, for they seem to know, as I do not, that there is no need for alarm.

September 28, 1998

There is a winsome quality to the way we absentmindedly skate across the surface of life, hardly ever peering down into its depth, and rarely even considering the miracle it is that we are here at all, alive, on our green and spinning planet.

We talk a lot about living in the moment, yet few of us actually know how to do this. How is it we repeatedly fail to notice the wonders surrounding us, and why do so many of us stumble through life with blinders on our eyes?

Perhaps it is an inborn human characteristic, part of our mammalian legacy handed to us from the apes. Or maybe it's a genetic trait, like blue eyes and red hair. It might be a biologic ploy to keep us safe and stupid, until a designated time when a sight or experience so singular and startling causes the blinders to fall away, and we see life clearly, for the first time.

That, I think, is our true religious awakening, a full-blown experience of being "born again" into full maturity, with the ability to discern and pay attention to the absolute miracle of life, in all its aspects, right here, right now, this very day.

October 2, 1998

What occurred at the hospital oncology clinic yesterday typifies the inadequacies of our current (mis)managed health care delivery system. We waited the obligatory three hours before being ushered into an examining room, since the hour of one's scheduled appointment bears no relationship to the time one is actually called to be seen. Once inside the exam room, Ted's blood pressure was taken, after which a nurse practitioner performed a perfunctory physical exam. She then left us alone in the cubicle to await the oncologist's arrival. While waiting, I thumbed through several old magazines stashed haphazardly in a plastic rack affixed to a wall, trying hard not to get angry about having to submit to this particular form of torture.

Almost an hour later, Dr. M appeared, sociable and friendly, attempting to engage us in lighthearted banter. Ted, gracious as always, was far more receptive than I. I had little interest in discussing trivia after waiting almost four hours. I was tired and anxious, so unlike my sweet husband, I somewhat curtly advised Dr. M that I preferred to learn the results of Ted's MRI to continuing our small talk.

Dr. M soberly informed us that the cancer had invaded Ted's spine, although no evidence of cord compression had been detected. He believed a short, intense course of radiation therapy would inhibit further tumor growth and alleviate any pain. Amazingly, Dr. M then informed us that an earlier MRI had also shown spinal involvement, but that he may not have mentioned it to us, at the time. It was last March, when Ted was so sick. Dr. M had paid scant attention to the relatively insignificant spinal findings when Ted's liver function was so precarious, and though he mused that he might have told us about it, perhaps he did not. There was so much else to worry about then, and as time passed, Dr. M had simply forgotten about it.

I understand why Dr. M felt Ted's spinal involvement was not clinically significant at a time when he was teetering on the verge of liver failure, but we should have been informed, and we were not. Of that, I am certain. I would never have forgotten such a significant finding. I am grateful for Dr. M's candor and his apology, and I'm confident in his clinical judgment, but I'm troubled by the environment in which he practices. The clinic staff and physicians are taxed to capacity, working doggedly, even heroically, but this overbooked clinic is a breeding ground for errors, and all too often such mistakes have important clinical consequences. Had we been aware of those earlier findings, it's possible that prompt intervention might have prevented or reduced the hip and back pain Ted is experiencing now.

October 7, 1998

Ted and I leave for New Mexico tomorrow, though sometimes I can't believe we're really doing this. It's more than a little odd to be traveling across the country to meet a Navajo medicine man who will perform a native healing ceremony for us, but Luke isn't only a medicine man, he's also a close friend of Karen's husband, Roy. They've been friends for years, and Luke wouldn't refuse any request that came from either Roy or Karen, though it's not his custom to share tribal rituals with outsiders. When Ted was so sick last March, at Karen's request, Luke performed a healing ceremony in absentia for Ted. It was shortly afterward that he began to dramatically improve. Did the ceremony help? Who knows, but it didn't do any harm, either.

My brother Joel has been urging us to visit Luke, noting that we have little to lose, so when Luke agreed to perform this ceremony, Joel provided us with first class airline tickets, and here we are, awaiting tomorrow's journey.

It would be easy to dismiss this whole idea as hocus-pocus, a primitive cultural practice left over from grander, if less enlightened times, had I not heard Karen speak of her own experiences with Native medicine. Karen, one of the most grounded, intelligent, and rational women I know, is convinced of its validity, and that makes me grateful for this opportunity.

Ted and I have no idea what to expect when we meet Luke, but when we decided to do this, we agreed to take it seriously, to behave respectfully, and to participate as fully as possible. Ted is quite excited. After teaching Native American literature for years, he's going to experience Indian culture for himself. I hope he isn't disappointed; I hope our journey goes well, but more than anything else, I hope this does some good.

October 8, 1998

Our trip to the airport quickly turned into a nightmare. We got Sophie and the cats to Susan and Alex's farm without incident, and were on our way to catch our 5:30pm flight with time to spare, but once we arrived at the airport things rapidly fell apart. Because of construction, the airport parking lots were closed, and the only available parking was at outlying park and ride lots. However, the posted signs failed to indicate that three out of four of those lots were also closed, so we spent almost an hour circling the perimeter of the airport until finally finding a spot in the back of the number four lot. It was, of course, the last lot we went to and the farthest from the terminal. We then waited another twenty minutes as two airport shuttles whizzed past us without stopping, but eventually we boarded a shuttle to the terminal and made our way to the airline gate. Ted was completely exhausted by this ordeal, but, as usual, he maintained his composure, and was kind and gracious to everyone he encountered. I, on the other hand, practically snarled at anyone in my path.

Our flight to Albuquerque was over booked and, unfortunately, our assigned seats were in the emergency exit aisle, where the seats don't recline. It would have been too uncomfortable for Ted to sit for three hours without being able to change position, so he switched seats, and we both sat next to strangers, instead of each other. Still, we were on the plane and on our way.

We made our connecting flight at Houston without mishap, and upon landing in the Albuquerque airport, we picked up our rented Buick Slylark, and made our way to a near-by hotel. Exhausted, we fell asleep as soon as we flopped down onto the bed. It had been a long, taxing day, but the next morning, refreshed and excited, we would drive to Farmington to meet Luke, and our real adventure would begin.

October 11, 1998

Last night, after returning to our hotel from Luke's house, following the completion of the healing ceremony, Ted traveled between two worlds.

His first visions appeared about half an hour after returning to the hotel. We were sitting on the sofa in our room, thoughtfully discussing the ceremony, when Ted asked what Sophie was doing here.

"Sophie's not here" I said. "She's home, where we left her, with Susan and Alex."

"No she isn't. She's right there, by the coffee table. Don't you see her?"

"Uh, no, I don't. Sophie's definitely not here, Ted. I think maybe you're hallucinating. I think whatever you smoked with Luke is doing weird things to your head."

"Really?"

Then came the vision of trains, buses, and trucks, and of people, too, all traveling in different directions to different places. When Ted told me about all this hustle and bustle, completely unperceived by me, I realized it was going to be a long night. I stood up, told Ted I'd be right back, and sprinted to the hotel bar, where I ordered four glasses of white wine, placed them on a round plastic tray, and carried them carefully back to the room. Under the circumstances, four glasses of wine seemed the minimum sustenance I'd need.

Ted told me he had traveled to the spirit world, and I drank two glasses of wine. He said that I had gone with him, that he had seen my spirit leave my body to accompany him, but I had experienced nothing. Ted claimed he went through a tunnel of light, emerging in the spirit world where he saw mosques, cathedrals, and temples. Although these buildings were of a religious nature, there was no dogma associated with any of them, they were simply beautiful, each in its own particular style. The buildings opened onto lush, scenic vistas, where children played, and clear water flowed in rivers, brooks and streams. Neither Ted nor anyone else was there as a reward for right living or for following a specific religious doctrine, but because this was simply the way life worked. There were animals in the spirit world, too, but Ted mainly noticed the beautiful spirit of the bull. He was, at some point, reunited with his mother's spirit; she was simultaneously the old woman he remembered as she lay dying, and the young woman he never knew, prior to his birth. It was, he later told me, a deeply moving experience.

Ted claimed he experienced a sense of total well-being in the spirit world and he wanted to go back again, to find his beloved grandfather. So, once more, he journeyed through the tunnel and came into the light, but he was unable to find his grandfather or anyone else he knew, although he noticed people dressed in striped costumes, acting as helpers and guides. Eventually, and with some reluctance, he returned to mundane reality.

Several times during the night, Ted threw up, sweating profusely. I finished the rest of my wine, and could have used a glass or two more, but, alas, the bar had already closed. Although Ted said he felt somewhat strange, he wasn't uncomfortable nor was he in any pain. He emphasized that the experience was not in the least bit frightening. On the contrary, he said he felt suffused with sensations of peace and joy.

Ted finally fell asleep, sleeping deeply the rest of the night, claiming in the morning not to have dreamt about any of his visions, but waking to feel refreshed and contented. He asserted that the visions he experienced the previous evening didn't have the qualities of a dream or a hallucination, nor had he felt stoned or intoxicated while experiencing them. He insisted that they felt "more real than reality," that they were not illusory, but that he had, with the help of a mind-altering substance, somehow crossed a boundary into another plane of existence, to experience a legitimate mystical episode. It was one of the highlights of his life, he asserted, fundamentally altering his understanding of the nature of human existence.

October 12, 1998

We drove from Farmington to Santa Fe yesterday, and today we spent a good deal of time strolling along Canyon Road, peeking into art galleries. Although Ted has had some back and hip pain, he's been able to move around relatively well, and he's thoroughly enjoying the art, especially the Native American pottery, which he's loved and collected for years.

Interestingly, in one art gallery we saw several Native American clown figures dressed in unusual striped costumes which Ted claimed were identical to the garb worn by the helper figures he had seen in his visions. It surprised him to see this, as he has no conscious memory of ever having seen such dress anywhere before his healing ceremony.

After a lunch of southwest cuisine at the *Coyote Cafe*, we walked to the *Indian Arts Museum*, where we saw several contemporary exhibits, each addressing the hardship of modern Native American life. There was a photographic exhibit of Indian teen-age mothers with their babies. Beneath each photograph hung a framed handwritten essay, authored by the young mom, describing what life was like for her and her child. The essays were deeply moving, occasionally sad, always insightful.

Another exhibit consisted of a glass teepee constructed from a variety of empty liquor bottles that was accompanied by scalding commentary referencing alcohol's corrosive and debilitating effect on Native communities. Yet another exhibit showed a sumptuous collection of feather fans, each one decorated with colorful and intricate hand-beading.

After returning to our luxurious casita at the *Alexandra Inn*, I watched an old but informative PBS documentary on American Indians, which seemed appropriate viewing for the occasion. We later went out to dinner at *Paul's*, a popular local restaurant, but Ted felt queasy and ate little.

I'm glad we fly home tomorrow. This trip has been wonderful for Ted, but I'm worried about him, and I feel insecure so far way from physicians, family and friends.

October 19, 1998

I can tell lots of stories about my horse, Lucky, or my adolescent bullmastiff, Sophie, or Atilla-Gorilla, and Asia, my two imperious kitties, but I'm fascinated by something more subtle than a cute story. I'm interested in something that seems a privilege, or a gift, or maybe, a lesson.

Lucky takes me places I might not go without him. I see a different world from Lucky's back as we move through terrain belonging to the deer, and the rabbit, and the owl. Debris collecting on the forest floor crackles differently under hooves, and there is something primeval about riding though lush, sun-dappled woods on a powerful and willing horse.

It's a joy to experience the world in this way, but on our best outings, there occasionally comes a moment when a boundary is breached, and the veil of otherness is briefly lifted. Lucky and I seem to merge into one being, as the experienced world dissolves, and I encounter a timeless bliss.

This has happened to me many times since the first time, but it isn't something I can force or predict, and it certainly isn't of my making. It might happen when Lucky and I come to a straightaway in the trail, and instead of walking on, I press my leg against his side to request a canter. He responds with a collected, cadenced, stride, and as the wind rifles my hair, I ask for more speed, and then, even more. Lucky shifts into each gait with the finesse of an Italian sports car, until we are galloping, flat-out, kicking up dust from the trail. Leaning slightly forward, I let the reins slip lightly through my fingers, grabbing a hank of coarse, gray mane. Time stops, as Lucky and I zoom down the tree-lined trail, freed from the bonds of time and incarnation, until the moment I lean back, and reclaim the reins. Lucky slows, first to a canter, then a jog, snorting and jigging, as pleased and exhilarated as I am.

This feeling of oneness comes to me most often in the presence of one or another of the animals I keep. It sometimes settles on me quietly when I look deeply into Tilla's golden eyes, or when Asia, curled in the curve of my lap, purrs a mantra that, like a prayer, fills the room with the sound of perfect peace.

Sometimes it happens after Sophie and I run down the grassy hill behind the house, meeting breathless on our dock, where we sit leaning against one another the way good friends sometimes do, silently contemplating the whole array of life the lake is home to.

These singular scraps of time, when the cloth of perceived reality is momentarily pierced, reveal a deeper reality. It is how I know, deep in my bones, that Lucky, Sophie, Tilla, Asia and I are integral parts of the web of Creation, and that we exist on this earth in relationship, to one another and all life.

October 28, 1998

I wish we had happier news to share with Charles and Susan when they arrive this weekend, but all we have is brutal, crisp reality. The cancer has spread rapidly, invading bone and causing Ted increasing discomfort in his hip and back. The chemotherapy, which had given us the gift of shared seasons, has ceased to be effective, and now we are looking into the hard, glittering eyes of this devouring beast; so we do our best. We hold hands and walk in faith toward a destiny that will not be circumvented. Death, or whatever transition we call by that name, will be the end of this. We know that. I will go with Ted as far as I can, though the time will come when I am forced to loosen my grip, let go of his hand, and watch him move from life into death's cool embrace.

This is the dreaded time as, little by little, Ted will slowly turn away not only from life, but from me. His body is hostage to this disease, taken over by mutinous cancer cells that demand total control of his body. I watch as he walks haltingly, his hesitancy wrenching my heart, and I find myself crying silently for the loss of his once exuberant stride.

November 16, 1998

I am distressed by the proximity of pain, illness, and death, yet all around me trees are dressed in party colors. Gold and crimson leaves tumble to the ground, swirling at my feet, falling to their fated destiny. I wonder if they fear it; death seems a casual thing in an autumnal context.

Secrets are carried aloft on autumn winds and coded messages are artfully inscribed on every falling leaf, but I have no ability to unravel these secrets. I don't know the vocabulary and cannot speak the language or spell such elusive words. Yet truths written in blood scarlet are conjured up whenever I plumb the deepest recesses of my own being, assuring me that the answers to my questions reside in every strand of DNA, and I need only trust my own beating heart to find them.

So this is what I know for sure, this is what I pull out when my hand reaches deep into the place where my soul resides: that death is the name we give to the mysterious rootstock of life. It is the old ending and the new beginning, the green bud of spring and the falling autumn leaf. It is the alpha and the omega, midwife to all life.

December 8, 1998

I don't recall the exact date Ted transferred from Duke Hospital to the inpatient facility of Triangle Hospice, but I know it was the Friday before Thanksgiving. I remember it was a Friday because I feared that if he didn't transfer that afternoon he would have to spend the week-end in the hospital, and that had become unacceptable.

Ted had been admitted to Duke Hospital for severe diarrhea caused by his out-patient radiation treatments. Dr. M, upon learning of the diarrhea, became concerned about dehydration, consequently, he advised admission to the oncology unit at Duke University Medical Center. Upon our arrival at the hospital, we walked from the admissions desk on the main floor to a bank of elevators that took us up to the oncology division on the ninth floor, where a nurse admitted Ted to his hospital room. At the time, Ted's pain was minimal, easily controlled with small doses of Oxycontin. The next day, Ted's diarrhea resolved but his pain began to increase, escalating steadily.

By his fourth hospital day, Ted was unable to move, even in bed, without severe pain deep in his legs, hips, and back. The oncologists sought to relieve it by increasing the dose and frequency of his Oxycontin and providing Oxycodone for breakthrough pain. It did little good. At my suggestion, they began an intravenous patient-controlled pump dispensing a morphine solution, but Ted's pain increased, nonetheless. I urged the doctors to increase the morphine dose but Dr. G, the attending oncologist on the unit, explained that a rebound effect could occur from increasing the morphine too quickly, causing it to lose all effectiveness. Consequently, ever so slowly, the dose was raised in tiny increments.

After several days, it became more and more difficult for Ted to endure the ever-increasing pain. Dr. D, the new attending oncologist on the unit (they changed weekly) ordered an MRI to determine the exact source of Ted's pain, but I insisted it could not be done until the pain was better controlled. Ted's excruciating bone pain made it untenable to transport him on a gurney to the MRI facility in a distant part of the hospital. Dr. D. agreed to increase his morphine dose to thirty milligrams an hour. Nevertheless, Ted writhed in agonizing pain upon attempting even the slightest shift of position in bed. He was unable to walk or stand, and finally, in despair, he asked me to take him home and help him die. In despair, I said I would.

In stunned desperation, I walked to the pay phone hanging on a wall in the hospital corridor and called Triangle Hospice. Several months earlier, I had initiated contact with them, and I thought perhaps they could help me determine what to do. I told their intake nurse that Ted was on the oncology unit at Duke Hospital in unbearable pain, and that I couldn't leave him there to suffer so.

"I wouldn't leave my dog here," I told her, "so unless you can offer a better alternative, I'm taking Ted home to do what he's asked."

Without a moment's hesitation, the nurse implored me to have him transferred immediately to the inpatient hospice. They could, she assured me, alleviate his pain. She explained everything I needed to do to effect a transfer that afternoon, promising they could do better than Duke.

"If we don't," she said softly, "then take him home, but I promise you, we will fix this if you give us a chance."

I returned to Ted's room and told him everything the hospice nurse had said. He agreed to the transfer. I then found Dr. D, still making his daily rounds on the unit, and explained that Ted wanted to be transferred to hospice that afternoon, that he could not, under these circumstances, spend the weekend in the hospital. Dr. D. was courteous and cooperative in facilitating the transfer, but I detected an edge in his voice, and had the sense he felt we were "giving up." Yet hospice was offering Ted a chance to meet his end with dignity and comfort. Oncologists sometimes construe their mission as a war against cancer, with death as the prime enemy, but I think the metaphor is incorrect. Death is neither an enemy nor a friend, it is the natural end of life, and it will come for each of us. There is no war, only the great and ever-rolling wheel of life and death. Hospice philosophy recognizes this, hence the patient isn't left to feel as though dying were a personal failure.

Ted has been here, in this home-like room, with handmade quilts and colorful paintings on the walls, for about two weeks. After his first day, his pain subsided substantially, and after three days, he was pain-free. Within twenty-four hours of admission, Ted was receiving more than twice as much morphine as he had been given in the hospital, in combination with several adjuvant pain medications, and he has consistently been alert, awake and able to read and converse. I learned from the hospice nurses that Dr. G was wrong about morphine, that large doses will not obtund a patient in severe, chronic pain, nor will it be inactivated by a rebound effect. Instead, it is sopped up by pain receptors the way water is absorbed by a sponge, allowing the patient to escape the burden of debilitating pain.

This facility is a lovely physical space, attractive and soothing, with splashes of color everywhere. Each individual patient room opens onto an outdoor patio, beyond which is a luxuriant meadow surrounding a pond that is home to ducks and geese. Bird feeders hang from shepherd hooks at each patio, so there are always sparrows, cardinals, and squirrels in abundance.

Now Ted is beginning to grow weaker. He's lost weight and resembles a pixie laying lightly atop the puffy air mattress. This week he has occasionally been confused, but there are other times when he's completely lucid, and still others when he appears to be speaking some strange, symbolic language I don't understand. His face has developed a beautiful radiance, and love emanates from him in an extraordinary way. He is often joyful, and always serene, projecting a deep peace. It is oddly beautiful, though, of course, I wish it wasn't happening. And I cannot imagine life without him.

December 9, 1998

The radiation oncologist who treated Ted during his last admission to Duke Hospital phoned me at home when he learned Ted was no longer there. He was genuinely concerned, wanting to know why Ted was no longer occupying a bed in the oncology unit. I explained that Ted's pain had increased dramatically within days of his admission, eventually becoming unbearable, and despite the doctors' best efforts, their attempts to subdue or even control the pain had failed. At that point, I told him, given Ted's general condition and prognosis, we decided to initiate hospice care. The radiologist was empathic, bemoaning the meager understanding oncologists have about how to alleviate chronic cancer pain.

"They just don't understand how to properly medicate chronic pain patients," he ruefully muttered, and I concurred wholeheartedly, launching into what had, by then, become my standard spiel on how narcotics bind differently to pain receptors in patients with chronic cancer pain, enabling them to handily tolerate narcotic doses that would kill an elephant.

The radiologist asked how much morphine Ted was getting, and when I responded he became very quiet, until finally asking in a small, thready voice if I was sure about that, if perhaps I didn't put the decimal point in the wrong place?

"No," I sighed. "He's getting eighty milligrams of morphine."

"Is he out of it?" the radiologist inquired.

"No, not a bit. When I left him, he was propped up in bed, contentedly reading *The New York Times*. Give him a call and talk to him yourself. He'd enjoy hearing from you."

The good doctor, utterly astonished by the amount of morphine dripping into Ted's vein, said he'd do just that. I hope he does.

December 14, 1998

I am distressed by the realization that Ted's experience at Duke Hospital is probably all too common. Oncologists, whom one would expect to know better, seem to have little understanding of how to treat severe chronic cancer pain. No one on the oncology unit, including the attending oncologists, had any idea how to relieve Ted's pain. Neither Dr. G nor Dr. D even came close to prescribing the large doses of morphine Ted required. Yet, upon his arrival at hospice, the nurses increased Ted's morphine dose substantially, and provided adjuvant pain medications, as well. Consequently, he became present and alert, able to participate in his own life within twenty-four hours of transfer.

It disturbs me to learn that one of the Duke oncologists routinely disparages the judgment and expertise of the hospice nurses. This doctor could learn a thing or two about pain control from them, but he's too puffed up with an inflated sense of his own knowledge and burdened with a bloated ego to pay attention.

I am not so impressed with the care Ted has received from this oncology group. They are smart, well-intentioned, and hardworking physicians all, but the volume of their practice is way too large, and consequently the care they render is sometimes sloppy. When Ted's back pain began in September, Dr. M attributed it to an increased production of digestive enzymes, rejecting my request for an immediate MRI. Yet, it came to light weeks later that bone metastasis had already been seen on a previous MRI, done months earlier. Had Dr. M not forgotten that, or if I had been informed of that finding when it was initially noted, I wonder if we might have prevented or, at least, minimized Ted's recent pain.

December 15, 1998

Ted looks like he is melting away as cancer overcomes him. His body is emaciated. Waxy, translucent skin stretches tightly over his prominent and knobby bones, and his muscle mass has been almost totally devoured by this disease. Yet, as his body shrinks, his spirit seems to grow. There is a beautiful radiance shining out from his face, and his smile, always sweet, has become sweeter still. It is an odd thing, but he seems swaddled in a crystalline light, and there is an unmistakable joy emanating from his bright blue eyes.

He is sometimes confused, talking nonsense, but there are other times when he's remarkably lucid, happily reading *The New York Times* in bed, or appreciating the integrity of Yeats's poetry. Sometimes, when he talks, though he makes no apparent sense, it seems as though he were speaking some symbolic language I don't know. Others have noticed this, too. My friend, Martine, and our minister, Robin, have both commented on it. He talks extensively of love, how beautiful the world is, and how fortunate he has been. Gratitude is his primary emotion. He is without bitterness, anger, or self-pity. Love for the world and gratitude for the gift virtually pour out of him. He talks about the journey that is life, and the adventure awaiting him as he passes from this world into the eternity of the hereafter, which beckons to him like a siren.

I am disconsolate knowing that each day he is closer to leaving me. I watch as he separates from all that is worldly and familiar, as he inches toward the precipice we name death, and I am left to wonder mutely how on earth I can stay behind and piece together a diminished life without him.

December 16, 1998

Last Sunday I decorated a six-foot Christmas tree in Ted's hospice room. I used our own ornaments and strings of colored lights purchased from Walmart, since I couldn't find our own white lights anywhere at home, and Ted has always liked the really flashy/trashy colored lights better, anyway. So here we are, with a fragrant and beautiful six foot blue spruce, a large pine wreath decorated with red balls and flashing white lights hanging on one wall, and a small "decorator" Christmas tree perched on a chair, winking light at Ted from across the room. We are ready for Christmas.

It will be a bittersweet holiday. I know it is my last Christmas with Ted, so it's hard to get in quite the right spirit. I certainly don't feel festive, yet I want to mark Christmas and not let it pass unheralded. It's important to acknowledge this sweet season, with its celebration of life and birth. Perhaps it's especially important this year, when I am too preoccupied by the thought and face of death, to notice the glow of a Christmas evergreen and how it illuminates dark places.

Charles and Susan are driving down from Ontario on Saturday with Desi hunched in the back seat of their little car. We hope to spend a quiet holiday at the hospice with Ted. There will be music, gifts, and great amounts of love. The sadness will be kept in check by flickering Christmas lights, the comforting aroma of pine, and Ted's ever radiant smile.

December 17, 1998

I arrived at hospice shortly before nine o'clock in the morning to find Ted already bathed and awake. He had the appearance of a frail wraith, cocooned in an oversized bed. His wavy hair, which has suddenly turned pearly gray, has grown long, forming a wild frame around his wizened face. He is tucked into brilliant white bed linens and wrapped in a bright white hospital gown, adding a tonal purity to his oddly angelic appearance.

As I walked into the room, he looked up at me, smiled, and told me how much he loves me, more than I can imagine, he warbled. He told me how wonderful it was to see me and how beautiful I looked. His Caribbean blue eyes gazed on me with adoration, and I felt my coronary arteries expand and my blood pressure drop a few points. It is impossible not to love this man. He had a good night and slept well, he said. The nurses took great care of him. He's a lucky man, he told me. I replied that he could have been a little luckier.

This afternoon Ted informed me he's ready to die. He's told me this before over the past few weeks. He is ready to take leave of life, and I suspect he's doing hard work toward achieving that aim. Meanwhile, I'm learning a lot about how one actually does die. It's not as simple as I once thought, the mere cessation of bodily functions. It now seems more complex, more subtle, and more mysterious. The body shuts down, to be sure, but there is also what one might call the mind, or the soul, or one's essential self that must also disconnect from this Created world, to be delivered into whatever it is that awaits us all.

December 19, 1998

I began reading *Anna Karenina* to Ted today. He asked me to read it to him so, slouching comfortably in the blue-plaid easy chair in his room, I opened the book and read the first several chapters. Ted listened attentively, a tender smile playing across his face. He loved it, he said. He loved me reading to him, and he loved the great novel. He was supremely happy, he said, and strangely, so was I.

I am wondering a lot lately about death and dying. Ted seems to grow in love and peace as time goes on, and I don't understand what I'm witnessing. It's an extraordinary thing, but now Ted seems almost entirely composed of radiance and love. The more wasted his body becomes, the stronger something I call his spirit, shines through. He is completely unafraid, certain that everything will be all right, that the Universe, or God or the Great Spirit will sustain him. I'm beginning to think he's right.

There has been too much beauty in his dying, too much peace, too much love, for me to think this is just an oddity. Ted talks of death now with sweet longing, as though he knows secrets I can only guess. It's a mystery for sure, but it leaves me to wonder about my perception of reality, and to question my certainty about the nature of life and death.

December 23, 1998

After returning home this evening, and playing several grueling rounds of tug in the middle of the living room with a happy and very energetic Sophie, I sat down at the dining room table, turned up the light, and cut the thirty-two diamond shapes needed to form the large Virginia Star that will be at the center of the quilt I'm making. The vibrant colors and jubilant prints are all in the richest tones of blue, green, and purple, with some black and white checked cotton thrown into the mix for additional zing. The colors and texture of these soft fabrics lift my spirits, and I'm glad to be making something beautiful and practical at a time when sadness threatens to overtake me.

The simple, repetitive act of piecing together this quilt top is comforting and meditative, giving me a sense of solidarity with generations of women before me who have turned ordinary remnants into hand-crafted treasures. These women have bequeathed a worthy legacy to me, a way to comfort myself by creating beauty, even in the midst of the most terrible sorrow.

December 26, 1998

Ted is becoming weaker. He wants to sleep more frequently, and he eats almost nothing. His body is fragile and bird-like, and I can almost see him departing this world in small but steady increments. He has been at hospice over a month now, far longer than I thought he would survive when we first arrived. Our time here, in its own way, has been remarkable. Ted has been virtually pain free, surrounded by the people (and bullmastiffs) who love him. He has been able to consider the whole arc of his life, savoring the fullness of it. Friends, colleagues, and students visit repeatedly, telling him sincerely how much wisdom and sweetness he has added to their lives. Charles, Susan, and I have each had time to say good-by, to express our love and to receive his.

We celebrated Christmas yesterday, a bittersweet experience, for sure. Ted sat in a chair during our gift-giving, which he thoroughly enjoyed. He received a white plush teddy bear, some chocolates, and a silver sculpture of a Canadian beaver standing at attention on a green granite pedestal. I got a quality rotary cutter and cutting mat for my quilting project and a lovely card inscribed with a poignant quotation from *The Little Prince* that Ted signed in a wavering script.

Martine arrived soon after Ted returned to bed, bearing a large lamb roast and a ragout of winter vegetables for Christmas dinner. Then our friends Valerie and Annie came with a dish of homemade cranberry relish. I contributed mint jelly and two bottles of chilled white wine, and Robin ambled in clutching an assortment of desserts and candles for the table. When Susan and Charles arrived with a gigantic bowl of garlic mashed potatoes we had all the makings of a real party.

The hospice staff joined in the feast, and Ted, delighted by the celebration, even downed a bit of wine. The rest of us ate and drank and talked and joked, putting sadness aside, as Ted's small hospice room filled with the cheer of the season. Even Sophie and Desi were given special Christmas bones to make their day festive too, and all the while, our two Christmas trees and lighted wreath twinkled and glimmered, scattering shards of color haphazardly on every wall.

December 28, 1998

I know that Ted will be leaving me soon. There is an unearthly quality to the extreme fragility of his body, and a ghostly translucence to his skin which is pulled tight across bones that stick out at odd angles. He seems weightless, as though he could soon float off the bed and evaporate, a wraith he is, a specter, a being made more from spirit than flesh.

He is dying, and I am dying, too. We are each dying to our old selves, only to be born again into whatever it is that comes next. Ted will undoubtedly be among the pantheon, one of those special souls lovingly transported by singing angels to the spirit world, or heaven, or somewhere over the rainbow. My next life is less clear, but it will surely be refracted through the lens of my relationship with Ted.

There are things I will need to remember, like the importance of a generous nature and the way kindness grows in an open heart. I will need to keep in mind Ted's quiet way, his dignity, and how he grew in love even as cancer grew in his belly and his bones.

I am learning things I hardly realize I'm learning. I'm discovering the deep-down meaning of life, known to those folks with sad eyes, whose arms wrap around my shoulders as they whisper that I need to let myself cry and trust my grieving heart. I am aware of that, I tell them. I will do those things, but the problem is that nothing I do will drop the sound of Ted's voice in my ear again, or give me the security I feel when his large hand clasps mine.

December 29, 1998

Each day now, I expect Ted to die. It's hard to understand how a body as frail and wasted as his can sustain life, but we are hardy creatures I suppose, and life is a persistent habit. Today Ted slept until mid-morning, awoke briefly, and then went back to sleep until Robin came by to visit in early afternoon.

Ted was delighted to see her and the three of us conversed for about an hour until Robin arose to leave, not wanting to tire Ted excessively. He immediately implored her to stay and continue the discussion, so we three talked for two more hours about life and death and the hazy space in between, which Ted appears to currently inhabit. Ted spoke of his reluctance to let go of life, how much he has enjoyed it, and how sad he is to be leaving this world. He is not yet ready to die, he told us, because life has been so sublime. He was perfectly coherent until something in his mind seemed to shift, and then his words made no sense, and he seemed caught between two possibilities, suspended in a middle place somewhere between life and death, shifting from coherence to babble, yet clearly seeking some sort of resolution.

Perhaps I'm reading too much into this, it's hard to tell, but I do know that Ted's face is aglow with an expression of joy and peace. It is a curious thing that's been commented upon by almost everyone who's seen him these past few weeks.

January 2, 1999

It's a new year but I have little joy in it; I know Ted won't live much longer. He is even thinner now, even weaker, and he has decided, I think, that it's time to let go, to break away from me and Charles and everything else still binding him to life.

He is sleeping almost constantly now, and when he's not asleep, he pretends to be. He doesn't want to talk and is ambivalent about whether or not he wants me with him. I think it's becoming distressing for him to see me and Charles, our presence making the inevitable more difficult for him.

He lies in bed, skeletal and slack-jawed, eye sockets sunk above bony cheekbones, breathing shallow, intermittent breaths that sound ominously like death. His body has a gaunt otherworldly appearance that reminds me of Christ on the cross, yet his ocean-blue eyes haven't lost their saturated color, and even now, at times, a winsome smile performs an arabesque across his face.

January 5, 1999

I arrived at hospice this morning to find Ted awake, alert and cheerful. He had been bathed, and the deep and necrotic bedsore at the base of his spine had been cleansed and dressed. Ted's appearance is disconcerting. He is emaciated and grimly skeletal. His skin is painfully thin, with raw areas of redness threatening to break down along each bony protuberance. Little by little, his tissues are dying. His color is ashen, with a definite blue undertone, evidence of his increasing circulatory compromise

Yet he was smiling when I arrived, and told me triumphantly that he had decided to live. He was worried, he said, that I would have a hard winter if he died, so he had changed his mind about dying. I told him that although I wanted him to live very much, I didn't want to burden him.

"I will be OK, even if you're no longer with me, you are part of my heart, now and forever, and that will sustain me," I whispered.

He listened, holding my hand in his still strong grip, then he kissed my lips and went to sleep. He slept most of the day, waking only for brief interludes. He is beginning to let go of life, in earnest. Perhaps he's being beguiled by some distant siren singing beautiful songs and promising everlasting love. He seems precariously balanced on the very edge of life.

Friday morning, January 8, 1999

Ted died at twelve thirty this morning. Charles and I were with him. Several hours earlier he had slipped into a light coma, yet his hearing seemed intact, so Charles and I spoke softly to him, at intermittent intervals. Mostly, we told him how much we loved him, and how, in the most meaningful way, he could never really leave us. He seemed peaceful and comfortable, swaddled in swirls of crisp white bed linens. The two Christmas trees and our little wreath filled the room with mellow, flickering, light, and Sophie, curled in a ball at the foot of Ted's bed, kept her own vigil.

About an hour before he died, while I was holding his hand, listening to the rasping sound of his labored breathing and thinking no thoughts at all, I suddenly heard myself asking,

"Is it beautiful?"

I have no idea what prompted this question, the words simply tumbled out of my mouth of their own volition, leaving me utterly surprised to hear them imposed on the surrounding stillness. Ted immediately snapped his eyes open, and they were as clear and blue as the Carolina sky on a sunny spring day. He turned his head slightly, so he was looking directly at me, then gazing deeply into my own wide open eyes, he answered in a robust voice, brimming with elation,

"Oh yes, it's very beautiful."

Then he closed his eyes, and less than an hour later, passed peacefully from this earth.

January 18, 1999

This is a strange time. I'm not sure I really comprehend that Ted has died, that I truly believe he will never stride through the front door of the house again, noisily shouting his arrival. It's an odd thing, and death is such a final state. It seems all wrong for Ted to be gone when I'm still here, so strangely solitary now, and not at all sure what to do with myself. Surely, we were meant to die together, holding hands as we jumped triumphantly into Eternity.

I miss him now with every breath I take. I miss everything about him, even the way he could be annoyingly fussy, even his tendency to be, at times, irritatingly professorial. I miss all his annoying little habits and would give anything to have him annoy me once again. And I am definitely unsure how to make a life that leaves out the wonder of him, all the integrity and decency that clung so effortlessly to him, the child-like delight, his love of language, the depth of his kindness.

He is part of me now. He is every act of goodness I perform, every generous thought I have, and all my impulses toward trust.

January 24, 1999

There are things I will not understand about Ted's death for a long time, but I know that it was a remarkable death and that Ted was a remarkable man. Although I loved him very much, I wasn't fully cognizant of his strength or his spirit before this illness came to us. Yet, the confident way he coped with cancer was, quite possibly, the most profound and loving gift he ever gave me, and he gave me many gifts.

I have been changed by the sorrow and the pain and the singular beauty of this past year. It has refined, burnished, and transformed me. I am a richer person, indeed. That being so, I would give anything to have my old life back, the sweet one I shared with Ted, before cancer took him away, changing everything, forever.

January 26, 1999

I miss Ted with a penetrating pain that leaves me exhausted and beaten, like a bloodied dog at the wrong end of a nasty fight. Trying to construct a life without him seems a Herculean task, and I'm hard-pressed to find worth in a life so diminished. Still, there's nothing else to do but get up every morning and try to find some joy in it, for in the final analysis, the best way to honor Ted's life is to value my own. It would belittle his desire to live fully right up to the end, if I throw my life away in a fool's fit of pique and despair.

Maybe it's really unimportant how long Ted lived or how many years we had together. Maybe the significant thing is that we were both alive at all, that we found one another here on this improbable, spinning planet, and that we loved each other with devotion, trust and joy. Maybe that's what matters most. I'm so grateful it happened, and were I given the choice to make all over again, knowing everything I know now, knowing exactly how it would all turn out, I'd do it again, happily, without a moment's hesitation.

January 27, 1999

It was warm today, more like May than January. Sophie and I went out early this morning, walking along the gravel road, down the big hill, and past the creek marking our property line. The creek is filled with clear, bright water, tinkling and gurgling as it rushes along, sounding like faerie music in a magical woodland. We followed the narrow path running parallel to the creek until it emerged by the lake, and then strolled the short distance to our dock. There, we sat ourselves down, bracing against one another, both of us gazing at the gently rippling lake. Suddenly, high in the sky, a great blue heron squawked loudly and dipped low just as he flew past us, perhaps in greeting to the only living beings in sight. We watched it fly up the narrow inlet, then veer left, towards the little pond by the red barn.

It was a special sight, reminding me that the richness of life is still present, and it's my responsibility to notice it and participate in it. Turning away from life, withdrawing in sorrow, would only give death a victory and denigrate the important lessons I've learned, but it's hard to be here without Ted and I will miss him until death unites us in timeless eternity.

In the meantime, life, like a magnificent rolling wheel, goes on, and so, indeed, shall I.

About the Author

Judith Harrow, a native New Yorker, has been an open-heart operating room nurse, a health-care risk manager, and a medical-legal strategist at a large metropolitan law firm. Now retired, she lives happily in North Carolina with an affable dog and two imperious kitties.

Made in the USA
Charleston, SC
15 July 2013